T0253006

SET MARGINS' # 11

INTRODUCTION
p. 4

1.
THIS SCHOOL IS A SANDBOX
AND THE WORLD OUTSIDE HAS NOTHING TO DO WITH IT

A.
MEETINGS TRANSCRIPTS
p. 14

B.
NO PROBLEM: DESIGN
SCHOOL AS PROMISE
(EXCERPTS)
Silvio Lorusso
p. 19

2.
I TRIED TO SUBVERT CAPITALISM WITH MY DESIGN PRACTICE.
NOW I'M LOOKING FOR A JOB.

A.
"THE SUBJECT SUPPOSED TO RECYCLE"
as explained by Mark Fisher
p. 32

B.
WHAT WE CAN'T DO
Afonso Matos
p. 33

C.
MEETINGS TRANSCRIPTS
p. 35

D.
SYSTEMIC CHANGE!
Afonso Matos
p. 43

3.
FRAMING DESIGN AS ART OR AS AN ONTOLOGICAL LIFE FORCE
IS ALL FUN AND GAMES UNTIL YOU HAVE TO PAY YOUR RENT :/

A.
MEETINGS TRANSCRIPTS
p. 48

B.
6 THESES ON THE
DEPROFESSIONALIZATION
OF DESIGN
Silvio Lorusso
p. 55

C.
TYPOGRAPHY, AUTOMATION
AND THE DIVISION OF LABOR
(EXCERPTS)
J. Dakota Brown
p. 57

D.
IF "LABOR IS ENTITLED TO ALL
IT CREATES", WHERE DOES
THAT LEAVE GRAPHIC DESIGN?
(EXCERPTS)
Interview by Somnath Bhatt with
Jack Henrie Fisher, Alan Smart,
Greg Mihalko and Danielle Aubert
p. 60

E.
NOT EVERYTHING IS 'ARCHITECTURE'
(EXCERPTS)
Marianela D'Aprile
p. 63

4.
WHAT IF DESIGNERS UNIONIZED...? HAHA JUST KIDDING... UNLESS......

A.
MEETINGS TRANSCRIPTS
p. 68

B.
POLITICS BEYOND DESIGN
Afonso Matos
p. 74

C.
WHAT COULD A UNION DO
FOR GRAPHIC DESIGN?
mixed materials by Evening Class
p. 76

D.
ABOUT THE INTERNATIONAL
TYPOGRAPHICAL UNION (EXCERPTS)
J. Dakota Brown
p. 78

RESPONSIBILITY BY THE EDITOR
p. 84

INTRODUCTION

Among a small but significant number of design institutions (mostly located in Europe, the US and the UK), a certain outlook upon the field has been taking shape. It has been given many names, but here we'll call it "Critical Design." This outlook perceives design as more than a market service: it aims to show that designers can be agents of powerful social and political change, beyond the boundaries of the commercial client-commission setting. From this perspective, designers are no longer meant to solve problems, but rather *frame* them. We are asked to shoulder the responsibility of *raising awareness* about the world's issues. We are encouraged to become provocateurs.

These apparently productive developments demand, however, some further investigation. Who can afford to do this type of critical work? What standard does it set for the remaining 99% of designers who must work for clients in order to pay their bills, many times bound to unregulated working conditions? Or is it that even those who do critical work are sometimes equally precarious? And that's not all. Beyond asking what the criticality discourse does to us, *designers*, we must also ask: what can it really do to the *world*? Are our critical projects changing anything or are they, ironically, doing the opposite and keeping the status quo intact? What are the limits of awareness-raising? Whose awareness is actually raised? By which visual and material means, and within which spaces?

CIRCLING AROUND THE CRITICAL

I enrolled in a Communication Design bachelor program blindly. I had never heard of it. I had been treading through a rigid path in STEM for the past three years of high school, and the escape that a so-called "creative" field posed was alluring. I had no idea what graphic designers did – even though I dealt with and consumed objects designed by them daily.

Even though I started my bachelor having almost no clue of what graphic or communication design was, I finished it thinking that design could be everything, everywhere. From the nowhere of invisibility to the nowhere of omnipresence, design's culture seems to stride between these non-places. It behaves like a force that is barely recognized by most people even though it shapes their lives. This cognitive dissonance is pervasive within the field, with designers claiming that "everything is design" and "everyone can be a designer" while at the same time trying to protect their profession from the gig economy, from platforms where you can order a poster online for 5 euros, from the menace of technological automation and from amateurs – those with no professional training who can become equally as good as formally trained designers, given the ubiquity of online tools, tutorials and software.

During my bachelor's degree, me and my colleagues benefited from quite experimental studio courses throughout the three years, where we could explore mediums such as sound, photography, video and installation art, while simultaneously having theoretical courses that aided conceptual thinking. We would both produce and design our content, content which would very often address various social, political and cultural issues. These social concerns were always present and we were encouraged to pursue them in our works, many times disregarding ideas of "good form" or "good design" in favor of a more thorough conceptual research, in favor of a pertinent message. This pleased me, given that I was quite passionate about activism – and silly young me thought that reading some theory and then doing a critical design piece addressing a social issue equated activism. When I learned that in this expanded view of design there was also a place for those urgencies, it felt like unearthing a treasure. I really loved my BA because of this. I could be *critical*.

Thinking in retrospect, this communication design programme, like many other European design programmes, seems to lean towards the third mode of criticality that Ramia Mazé ascribes to design practice in her contribution for the publication *The Reader* (2009).[1] In the text, Mazé proposes three different modes of criticality within design. The first is an individual designer's criticism towards their own personal practice. The second relates to criticism towards design in general, to its methods, culture, frameworks and dogmas. Then, the third mode relates to the

[1] Included in the *lapsis Forum for Design and Critical Practice*, which also gave rise to the exhibition *Forms of Inquiry* (2007) at London's Architectural Association.

cases in which design addresses urgent social and political issues. Here, in contrast to the previous modes, design itself isn't so much the object of criticism as it is the vector through which this criticism is directed elsewhere. We can witness this framework at play in a whole gamut of recent approaches, sporting names like Social Design, Speculative Design, Design Activism, Design Fiction, Contextual Design, all of which could vaguely fit under the umbrella of this third modality.

A similar formulation to Mazé's definition can be found when Els Kuijpers talks about productivism, in her proposal for a spectrum of strategies within communication design.[2] Kuijpers puts forward a set of five nomenclatures – functionalism, formalism, informalism, productivism and dialogism – which she argues are not *"meant as a historical classification of styles with distinguished ideological positions but as a flexible scale in which the designer constantly shifts – depending on the circumstances."* Productivism, according to Kuijpers, *"puts communication design at the service of a social programme aimed at bringing about change in society."*[3]

The research object of my Master thesis (or at least its starting point) was defined along these lines, and I simply called it Critical Design.[4] This name serves as a container for all those approaches that – following Kuijpers' and Mazé's definitions – aim to use design as a vector for social critique and social change, and, perhaps more importantly, see the designer as a political actor, an agent whose work is perceived to have a certain *power* upon our lived environment. Under this banner I could include many instances, for example, most of the projects produced within schools such as the Design Academy Eindhoven or the Sandberg Instituut's Design Department (as well as their pedagogical ethos); design studios such as The Rodina or Dunne & Raby; events like the Forms of Inquiry exhibition or

[2] Kuijpers, E. (2016). *Style? Strategy! On Communication Design as Meaning Production* in Laranjo, F. (2017). *Modes of Criticism 3 — Design and Democracy.* Eindhoven: Onomatopee. pp. 19

[3] Upon talking with Els, I understood that it isn't possible to ascribe so closely the notion of Productivism to Critical Design as a whole. She actually aligns some Critical Design projects more with her notion of Formalism: a spectacle of form, but lacking in conveying any message through that form.

[4] Critical Design was coined by product design duo Dunne and Raby in the late 90s. They define it as follows: *"Critical Design uses speculative design proposals to challenge narrow assumptions, preconceptions and givens about the role products play in everyday life. (…) It is more of an attitude than anything else, a position rather than a method."* In this booklet, the usage of Critical Design starts off by encompassing this definition, as well as Mazé's and Kuijpers' contributions to it, but the aim is not so much to focus on theoretical definitions of what Critical Design is or isn't, but rather to examine its effects upon the profession, as well as its origins.

the Istanbul Design Biennales; publications like Keller Easterling's *Medium Design*; or micro-polemics such as the ones that stemmed from the *Republic of Salivation* project at MoMA's *Design and Violence* exhibition.

Such critical practices define design as more than a service industry. They stem from research programmes, from funds and grants, from positions within academia – either as students, tutors or researchers – or just as the result of an "independent" practice (as in, independent from clients). However these approaches do not necessarily circulate outside the market, but instead within an exclusive market of their own. In their eager criticism of the workings of the outside world, these projects often forget to examine the socio-economic conditions that enable their own existence. How are they financed? Who can afford to uphold this dream of creative and critical autonomy after graduation? And also: Where do these projects circulate? Who gets to engage with them? What does that engagement lead to?

WHAT IT DOES TO US AND
WHAT IT DOES TO THE WORLD

I finished my Bachelor in Lisbon with a "speculative design" project: a fiction that proposed an alternative reality where humanity had evolved to become a collective hivemind. This was a group project, done with my friends Inês Pinheiro and Vítor Serra. As proud as we were of our project, when we looked at the maximalist aesthetics and cloudy, lyrical language it employed, we couldn't help but pose two simple but grave questions to ourselves: "*What can something like this really do to the world?*" and "*How can someone make a living doing projects like this?*" Still, today, I believe the essence of these questions – as simplistic and naive as they were – is one worth pursuing. I believe it's within these two questions that we can find the two barriers Critical Design faces: on one hand, the relevance that it can have to society and on the other hand, the feasibility of its practice for each designer. Somewhat rephrased, those two questions became the foundation of my research: *Who can afford to be critical? And what can criticality afford?*

8

Asking two questions allows for a dual analysis. The first investigation highlights matters of privilege: Why does it seem like Critical Design is exclusive to a minority of designers who can conduct self-initiated, independent, critical projects, while the great majority of the profession doesn't have the choice to do so? The second question focuses on the impact that critical discourses on design have upon the real world, outside of the profession – and on the very origin of the urge to have an impact on the world. Does Critical Design exist because designers want to use their skills to enact progressive social and political change? Or are there other historical contingencies that can explain this almost philanthropic drive? Is there a hidden (or better, subconscious) agenda?

At this point, it became clear to me that the age-old concern regarding *what we can do to the world as designers* is what fueled my research. If we can do something, will it be through Critical Design projects that target social and political issues? Or will it be through a different way of being critical, maybe one where criticality is directed towards the field itself, in hopes that by reflecting on design's own mechanisms we might understand how they already impact the world? In other words, can one craft a critical practice of design, which is different from Critical Design? Or would such a critical practice limit our agency even more? What is the relation between design's *power* and the designer's *agency*? What if instead of discussing how to impact society with our designs, we discussed first how we can impact our own world – our own field, one teeming with competition, precariousness and professional insecurity (of which Critical Design itself might be a symptom)?

These matters were explored throughout my second year at Design Academy Eindhoven's Information Design MA. Even though it was, to some extent, quite challenging, my time at DAE also ended up being extremely joyful. I met some of the most wonderful people, had the nicest conversations, went to some of the coolest parties in the weirdest places, cycled endlessly, had daily dinners with my best friends, and tapped into a kind of life so different from the one I was leading in Portugal.

However, I was also acutely aware of the privilege I had to be there. This kind of romanticized "European citizen" experience is one that is still a faraway mirage for many young people my age. I was able to enjoy this time because I'm lucky to have a mom, a dad and grandparents supporting me financially. And this luck that I had was not shared by many of my peers, like those who had to fully fund their studies by themselves with several part-time jobs, or like some non-European students who had to start GoFundMe campaigns to be able to afford their Masters. I'm mentioning this not as virtue signaling, but rather as a simple act of transparency — so that the reader knows that, when browsing through those pages, what financed my masters and this booklet was not an independent critical design practice or cool design jobs. What enabled this book to exist was my family's, as well as Freek's (founder of Set Margins') personal financial investment in it.

One of the things that set my research in motion was exactly how I (and many others) found DAE to be so (intentionally?) oblivious to the clear reality that their students, in order to study there, had to pay their tuition fees somehow. So, if we start examining many of DAE's values (and of Critical Design in general) under the lens of money, of affordability, many things start to transpire this almost instutionalized, subconscious avoidance — not only regarding the present conditions of their student body, but perhaps even more regarding the future they will face once they graduate.

For instance, when the school claims to be forming *"generations of designers who believe they have the power to make a difference,"*[5] is it not sidelining the very real material constraints which curb one's power? Is it not ignoring matters of money, of class, and the fact that design is, in general, work? Because as long as design is work, designers are, most of the time, dependent on someone else to pay for their labour, and thus must abide by their demands. So, while inside these schools we get to decide what it is that we're going to make *and* we also get to make it, this flattening of the hierarchy[6] between power (decision-making) and labour

[5] Description from an Instagram post on DAE's official account, quoting writer and Dezeen editor-at-large Amy Frearson. Posted 01.03.2022. Retrieved from https://www.instagram.com/p/Caj0PBNAKkl/

[6] Lorusso, S. (2021). *Design and Power - Part 1*. in Other Worlds #4.

(production) rarely happens outside of this educational context. That is a simple fact of capitalism, but one which seems to be often overlooked in Critical Design circles.

In order to take these matters out of the pages of my thesis and into reality, I defied my introvert self into organizing a series of meetings with DAE students, where we set out to discuss how work, money and precarity limit the efforts of pursuing critical design practices. We met from February to May 2022 and discussed many things regarding (critical) design schools and (critical) design work. These conversations were recorded and the excerpts were grouped under 4 main themes:

1. The bubble of the (Critical) Design School;
2. The power of design and the agency of designers;
3. The nature of design (as a profession? Or more than that?);
4. Collective power.

These themes gave rise to 4 zines that are now edited together inside this book-container. This object you now hold gathers bits of my thesis, excerpts from our meetings, texts by invited authors (and also a selection of memes which perhaps add more to this discourse than my words ever could!). This book is born mainly from my own personal admiration for the design researchers and meme-makers that gave me the tools to express feelings, doubts and anxieties for which I had no words yet. Ever since I found the texts and images you encounter in these books, I've wanted to share them with everyone I know, and I'm really happy that I now have the chance to do so. I'm also greatly indebted to all my friends and colleagues from Design Academy who were similarly concerned by these topics and shared their extremely relevant thoughts and opinions. I hope these multiple materials can bring novel perspectives into a field which, ironically, doesn't need any more novelties.

THIS
SCHOOL IS
A SANDBOX
&
THE WORLD
OUTSIDE
HAS
NOTHING
TO DO
WITH IT

1.
THIS SCHOOL IS A SANDBOX
AND THE WORLD OUTSIDE HAS NOTHING TO DO WITH IT

On the bubble of the Critical Design School.

This chapter concerns the gap that exists between the reality of Critical Design Schools (such as Design Academy Eindhoven) and the reality of work. It aims to question the promises that the school puts forward, or, as Silvio Lorusso puts it, the *"myth of autonomy and self-determination."* Who can afford to be critical? Who can continue doing the same kind of research projects once they're done with their studies? What are the financial conditions that allow some to do critical work where they see *"design as research"* or *"as authorship"*, while others must engage in commercial jobs, under a *"design as service"* model — many times working under precarious, unregulated conditions? Or is it that even those who do critical work, and who *seem* to afford to do it, are in the end equally precarious, to various degrees? Is there an outside to precarity?

INDEX

A.
MEETINGS TRANSCRIPTS
p. 14

B.
NO PROBLEM: DESIGN
SCHOOL AS PROMISE
(EXCERPTS)
by Silvio Lorusso
p. 19

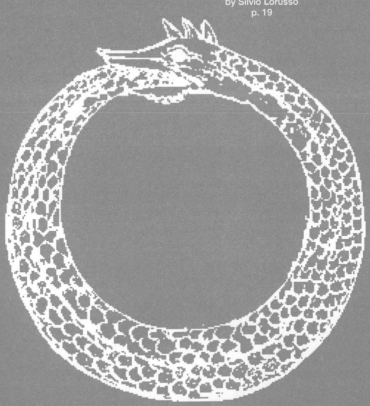

A.
MEETINGS TRANSCRIPTS

Some students from DAE got together to talk about class, finance, precariousness and the intersection of those themes with the realities of the critical design world and of the critical design school. The excerpts below are mostly extracted from the 2nd meeting of this group, with some remarks coming from the 1st session. On the 2nd meeting, the text *No Problem: Design School as Promise* (see pg.19) by Silvio Lorusso was read and discussed.

MEETING NO.2 — 17/02/2022 — 17h30-19h30

M.P.

I was thinking, **is it possible to be critical outside of this school?**

Like, we were talking about that...Maybe for us there is not a lot of space to make these things.

A.M.

Is there a space? Yeah, I think that's kind of the crux of it... because, I mean, some of us can still continue to do this if we get access, for example, to systems of funds and research grants. That's one way to fund it. We could actually talk about the financial means through which one can sustain a critical practice, in order to understand who actually can afford to be critical and who can't. So that's one way:

the fundings, the grants.

B.M.

It's a bit unrealistic — to project what we're doing now on the outside. Also, obviously you talk with people that finished, or people that had similar experiences in other countries... And they end up doing either very different things, or things related to a client-based type of work. So, for sure, this experience opens a lot of possibilities, and it's a very introspective path somehow. But then to project this methodology we use into the future...I'm like...Hm, Hm...No.

I.P.

I think one way of being able to sustain it is to become really famous. [laughter] And I think that's also what motivates the individualization and atomization of designers, I think. That's why everyone tries to be so unique.

G.D.A

To fit THE STAR DESIGNER.

14

V.S.
I also feel like there's a sense that, if you "make it", that there's something exceptional about you. There's this sense of exceptionalism, I think, and this also drives away the focus from what material conditions allowed you to do that, or maybe that sometimes you look like you made it, but in truth you're actually still precarious in other ways. (...)

MEETING NO.1 — 10/02/2022 — 17h30-19h30

M.B.
I've already been through a graduation show here. And among the people with whom I graduated, there were some Cum Laude. And they've had a shit situation afterwards. Like, there is the image that you build that, if you get the

Cum Laude

, and/or if you get published by Dezeen and so on, that you are going to have success. And indeed, you see that some Cum Laude people and some not Cum Laude people get massively published in those media...but they have no work. Being visible doesn't mean that you will get a stable, non-precarious practice.

I've also worked for a studio in Sweden where they would get in all these publications, like Elle Decoration, and they would get awards and so on... And I was like: *Wow, you must be so proud.* And they were like: *We don't care. This doesn't bring projects. This doesn't bring food on the table.* So it's also about understanding that within the design field there are all these sorts of delusions about visibility and media attention. But that's not what makes your practice sustainable. (...) I just wanted to highlight the difference between *actually* making it and *the image* that you made it.

V.S.
I think it's like: one thing doesn't invalidate the other. I think it adds insult to injury. It's already bad enough that there's some incentive to work in an individual way, because you might get the Cum Laude, these honors that set you apart from the others. It's even worse because you get those things and then you're actually just as better off as everybody else. It adds insult to injury, I guess.

And that's the thing. Then, once you try to keep going with the same practice, after you leave school, and you don't make it, what happens to you? What do you have to do afterwards in order to survive?

I.P.
You continue studying.
[group laughs]

V.S.
But like...if you have to finance your studies!

I.P.
You go work in a restaurant!
[group laughs again]

V.S.

Yeah, you are probably gonna end up having to work a part time job, perhaps even for a big corporation. You're still going to be exploited or you're still going to perpetuate this exploitative system the same way. It feels like, instead of trying to jump all of these hoops through the school, and through the graduation and through the Cum Laude and then not having anything, to get to that point where you finally have no other option other than do that type of labor, you could just commit to it and say, *"I'm going to eventually have to do this type of labor. I might as well try to organize while I'm doing it. Organize with people that are in the same position as me, to change our collective condition when we're in this position."*

back to... MEETING NO.2 — 17/02/2022 — 17h30-19h30

A.M.

I'm reminded of how Joost, our head of department, runs his studio, like, the economic model they use. Essentially, the studio sustains itself, he told us. He has enough money to pay his employees and to sustain the activity of the studio, but then he doesn't take any money for himself from there.

I.P.

But his personal income comes from teaching only...so, when I said before that you could sustain yourself if you become famous, that's actually not true. You could say Joost and his studio are quite well known, but still he has to do something else, he has to have a job in teaching.

A.M.

But that's the thing. Earning a living from doing just "Critical Design", or a kind of design where you can actively have a certain level of freedom and agency, even just agency in choosing the projects you accept — it's not a thing. You always have to sustain yourself with some other job. Even if it's teaching, even if it's teaching at a Critical Design School —

V.S.

— and then there's not space for everybody to do that, to be teachers —

A.M.

— and that's like, the most insidious. Because it becomes a pyramid scheme (of sorts).

It's like: you're teaching others critical design. And then, the only way for them to continue in that medium is for them to become teachers themselves, who *then* go to teach more people that the only way for them to do this is to be teachers! And so on...

[group laughs]

G.D.A

That's why this school is full of designers, but not educators. Like, there are few educators around here that think pedagogically in a certain way. The rest are designers. Those things are different.

A.M.

That's also an interesting point. Sometimes you do have the experience that certain tutors are not necessarily good tutors. They're good designers, but they might not be the best people at teaching or being educators.

MT.B.
That's why teaching is sometimes a separate career! [laughs]

GROUP
Yeah, yeah.

A.M.
Here they're just like, "*okay, you're a good designer, don't you want to do this freelance teaching gig for six months?*" Which is also precarious for them!

I.P.
And for us, because we can end up doing the same!

C.M.
I feel like in our department there are a lot of tutors that are coming out of the department itself. So, for example, all of the workshops are done by previous Information Design students...And that is a good thing because it's giving the "future us" some opportunities, but at the same time, it's this...

...*SNAKE THAT IS EATING ITS OWN TAIL.*

17

meme by
criticalgraphicdesign.tumblr.com

S.T.
I think that what worries me is that there is no market for critical design.
And maybe there is not even a public for it. So maybe you're working your
ass off in order to get some money to do your critical practice, and then
there's actually no one to listen to it apart from your peers.

G.D.A
And when they ask you *"What are you gonna do now? Are you gonna go back to
your own country?"* And the answer that I have is like...

you don't even speak the same language anymore.

Like, it's not that there is not a market, it's that it's almost like you no
longer speak the same language. I mean, many of us are gonna stay...maybe
not in Eindhoven...but in the Netherlands...Because we are kind of forced
to stay here within these institutions...

V.S.
...if we want to do the same type of work, yeah...

C.M.
To be honest, personally, the way I took this education so far, and also
the moment I decided to go through with it was by thinking: I will do things
that will give me skills and methods and ways of thinking that then I will
employ in another kind of business sector, which is the one that is more
client-driven. But then I don't know if I'm thinking like this because that

is something I'd *like* to do, or because this is the only thing that I think I could *possibly* do. Like, I already put a limit on myself, even before starting, saying, *"okay, don't think that you're gonna do this for real."*

A.M.
But I think that kind of realism can sometimes be productive. Because that doesn't necessarily mean that you're betraying your ethics or your values. We all grapple with that or are struggling with that to some extent. Like: to what extent are we "selling out", or just giving in to a commercial practice? "Just" doing service design? We feel like we're betraying the values and the critical thinking that we just acquired...

But that's also why I don't think that the last horizon of criticality is design. It's hopefully not. If you can't be critical through your job, through the thing that earns you money, that doesn't mean that you are less capable of being political or being critical beyond that.

I.P.
Also, I think that the school should be a place for experimenting and trying out things that you cannot try out outside of school. And I think that's also good. It's a safe space where you can do the things that you want to do. But it's more like..the problem is the lack of transparency. It's the *Promise* that is the problem. The lack of realism.

B.
NO PROBLEM: DESIGN SCHOOL AS PROMISE (EXCERPTS)
Silvio Lorusso

published in
Entreprecariat

December 7, 2020

In this text, designer and researcher Silvio Lorusso talks about the (Critical) Design School as the locus of a specific kind of promise. He goes on to characterize what this promise entails and what happens when the promise isn't fulfilled — what kind of feelings arise on the promisees (the students)?

THE PROMISE

A promise is something that is put forward. It involves intent and expectation. It is a performative speech act: an utterance that, hopefully, does what it says. A promise is fulfilled when an intended future, now become past, finally aligns with the present. That's when the speech act meets its condition of felicity.

What kind of promise (from now on simply "the Promise") does design education involve? Does that relate to the present of education or to the future of work? What are the forces that shape it? How is it fulfilled and by whom? Who has the authority to sanction its fulfillment? Let us consider educational promises in general. First, they are not unilateral but reciprocal. It is not just the *promisor*, namely the school organization, in cooperation with or in opposition to the market and society, that is supposed to fulfill it ("We'll give you knowledge, skills and a space to develop them"), but the individual *promisee* as well, the student, as they guarantee effort and participation ("I'll make it worthwhile").

Things get easily complicated because the Promise is not unambiguously formulated—there is no clear contract—and yet it looms over the promisee, functioning both as encouragement and threat. It can be rooted in notions like success, career, self-realization, ambition, autonomy... But, it can also aim at redefining them. It is affected by geography, class, race and gender. It comes in multiple shapes and forms and yet it can be understood as a whole. Does the Promise resemble a vow, an oath, a resolution, a mission? Is it as nebulous and frail as the American dream? In the design field things get even more complicated, as the field itself is in perennial reconfiguration: it experiences a constant identity crisis, some might say, fueling the personal identity crisis of practitioners.

To focus on the Promise means bridging preexisting societal conditions—such as employability, welfare, housing availability, discrimination, mobility, privilege—with socialized professional and personal aspirations—lifestyle, institutional roles, legacies of crafts, research trends, urgent matters, subcultures, notions of virtuosity... In other words, the Promise is built on some premises, at once materialistic and idealistic. When there is no full alignment between a promise and its premises, the promisee feels like they are compromising. From this a question arises: who is defaulting when the Promise is not fulfilled? And what can be claimed as compensation? (...)

THE SCHOOL

To be sure, the design field is vast and diverse, and so are design schools. What I want to focus on here is the kind of design school that isn't uncomfortable with being associated with art: by indicating the fruitful relationships between the fields and their historical entanglement (think of the tradition of applied arts), I am interested more in the design schools that belong to the art academy than in those that are associated with architectural and engineering departments. This doesn't fully solve our framing problem, though. So, my strategy will be to consider not a singular institution, and

Designer

A S

Administration Support, Barista, Bartender, Busser, Cashier, Customer Service Representative, Cook, Credit Controller, Data Entry Clerk, Event Promoter, Delivery Driver, FAST FOOD ATTENDANT, Fast Food Chain Crew Member, Fitness Trainer, Inbound Call Center Representative, Labourer, Mail Sorter, Office Clerk, Payroll / Expenses Assistant, Pick-Packer, Mail Carrier, Receptionist, Sales Floor Team Member, Sandwich Artist, Telemarketer, Telephone Marketing Researcher, Valet, Wait-staff

Generously Funded Multi-Disciplinary Critical Unskilled Praxis	Zero Hour Reading Room Inquiry Self-Initiated Exploitation Reflexive Benefits	Explores the 'mise en abime' of the designer itself

meme by
criticalgraphicdesign.tumblr.com

not even a series of them. Instead, I will focus on the School. The School is an "ideal type", a useful fiction that, for the sake of the argument, combines, isolates (and maybe exaggerates) traits of the actual institutions I observed by means of direct involvement or distant scrutiny. Whereas the Promise is real, although vague, the School is unreal and yet derived from actual cases.

These cases, which are mostly concentrated in the urban nerve centers of the Netherlands (as well as being linked with the UK and the United States) are definitely a minority and don't represent design education at large. However, they perceive themselves, and are often perceived, as a sort of avant-garde. Embodying newness, the School suggests directions to other organizations, both educational and professional. The School, supported by a generous system of public funds, can legitimately consider itself a site of reflection, cultural production and renovation. Admittedly, its novel culture is not passively accepted by the field at large, instead it is often confuted, adversed, or simply ignored. And yet, this culture influeznces the field. Whereas the School has the means to make a cultural idea visible to the field, it is not hegemonic and doesn't want to be, at least ostensibly. The School doesn't say "design should be this or that", but it presents itself as the locus of doubt and experimentation. Certain ideas grown within the School will leak out in the field at large, through the practices of its alumni, through final shows, through textual production and debates later hopefully cemented into design history. But also through the mockery, skepticism and disdain of its detractors. In a 2011 essay, Rob Giampietro pointed out that the culture of design was becoming increasingly like the schools' culture. The School is the laboratory where this very equivalence is produced. So, reverting the postulate, talking of the School means talking of the culture of design.

AUTONOMY

(...) The Promise is [also] one of autonomy and self-discovery. However, this process is rarely tied to material constraints. When urging students to become who they are, the School developed only a partial alertness and sensitivity: it is rarely concerned with class, census or wealth. Talk on professional exploitation and self-exploitation, increasingly high fees, little pay, unemployment, unfair working conditions, uneven funding possibilities, expiring visas, etc... in one word, precarity, is still infrequent. As it is infrequent to point the finger at the most obvious power disbalance within educational institutions: on the one hand, the powerful managerial class (the stable organogram) and on the other, the fragile teaching staff, whose members are occasional and redundant. Instead, successful stories imbued with survivorship bias are foregrounded.

To avoid misunderstandings, let me say this loud and clear: all the dimensions of inequality are equally important. Not just important, *they're real* and inextricably linked. A School that is explicity anti-racist and non-patriarchal is also, by default, against precarity. If that thing we call progress actually exists, this is where we see it.

An emphasis on precarity is much needed as it counterbalances the myth of life and career self-determination that can be fuelled by a simplistic idea of autonomy and self-direction. An emphasis on inequality would foreground what is statistically hard to achieve and what aspects of practice are strictly dependent on local possibilities. In other words, to what extent society determines biography.

I suspect that a miopia towards professional limitations results from design and designers' protagonism (more rarely, from a solid and remunerative career). What matters is the mark that the designer leaves on the world, not the scar that the world leaves on the designer. Professional disadvantage might sound gloomy, depressing, almost a petty subject. A workshop on precarity? Not fun. Surely, the School doesn't want to sadden its students. And yet, workshops on entrepreneurship abound. Is there a way to lead their interest to these topics without curbing their enthusiasm? This is the dilemma that the School, usually proud of its criticality, must address if it wants to be considered fully critical.

FUTURE

To what extent is the School actually attentive to the future? The temporally and geographically distant, and therefore safe, canned futures of speculation are favored over the tedious and mundane present-like pseudo-future of life-after-graduation. Again Papanek: "*It is also in the interest of the Establishment to provide science-*

fiction routes of escape for the young, lest they become aware of the harshness of that which is real." As this prospect is grim in the most unspectacular way (this is what makes it terrifying), the School recasts the Promise as something oriented to the present: a promise of space and time, protected from the idiotic frenzy of the work grind. In fact, several students arrive at the School *after* years of professional activity.

Present-orientedness makes sense: if the School is truly a site of cultural production, what it has to offer are mostly the relationships that take place within its shelter. Not cultural production, then, but the production *of a* culture. Some would call this "prefigurative politics", a sort of controlled experiment that is meant to be later implemented on a larger societal scale. If this is the case, the issue of individual sustainability should be central. Exiting the sandbox, would the student fall into an abyss?

This is the humble urgency that even students themselves tend to postpone to the last months of education (if they are not preoccupied with things like visas), in favor of more epic and apparently noble urgencies dictated by the agenda of the museum-festival complex. One does not even have to wait for graduation to encounter the unfashionable urgency of circumstances. A proof being the crowdfunding campaigns to afford concluding one's studies in cities with rocket-high rent and a housing crisis, or even beginning these studies in the first place! A new "design challenge" is getting traction: craft a GoFundMe to sustain your design studies in a fancy cultural hub.

Adversarial Design Interrogative Design
Contestational Design Medium Design
Critical Design Ontological Design
Design Fiction Open Design
Design for Debate Participatory Design
Design Justice Pluriversal Design
Design Thinking Post-Capitalist Design
Disarming Design Posthuman Design
Discursive Design Reflective Design
Disobedient Design Responsible Design
Eco-Social Design Social Design
Empathic Design Speculative Design
THE TERRAFORMING
Ethical Design Transformation Design
Future Design Transition Design
Undisciplined Design
Human-Centered Design

Contextual Design

GEO-DESIGN

meme by
@ethicaldesign69 (FKA @neuroticarsehole)

I tried to subvert capitalism with my design practice.

Now I'm looking for a job.

2.
I TRIED TO SUBVERT CAPITALISM WITH MY DESIGN PRACTICE.
NOW I'M LOOKING FOR A JOB.

On the power of design and the agency of designers.

What can we, designers, do? This chapter concerns the urge that many designers feel to engage with social, political and enviromental issues through their work. It also concerns two different ideas which are rarely scrutinized separately, as if they mean the same thing: the power of *design* (as a world-encompassing system which permeates all aspects of our lives) and the power of *designers* (as individuals). But what power do we actually hold? Should we be talking about power, or about *agency*? Who is the individual designer who is in place to do such a thing as "systemic change"? When does a designer, usually responsible for the *making*, for executing orders, also has the capacity to *decide what it is to be made*? And, if "*great power equals great responsibility*," what type of power and what type of responsibility are we talking about, when we talk about our design practices?

INDEX

A.
"THE SUBJECT SUPPOSED TO RECYCLE"
as explained by Mark Fisher
p. 32

B.
WHAT WE CAN'T DO
thesis excerpts by Afonso Matos
p. 33

C.
MEETINGS TRANSCRIPTS
p. 35

D.
SYSTEMIC CHANGE!
thesis excerpts by Afonso Matos
p. 43

designacademyeindhoven "DAE has produced a generation of designers who believe they have the power to make a difference"

If designers don't think about and practice design at the level of systems and put politics at the core of what they do—with climate crisis, fascism, racism, xenophobia—when we realise that we don't have any other option, there will be no future at all.

ok but how do we practice design at the level of systems??

can we??????

', designers can take hold of, dismantle, and rewire some of the abusive structures of capital by manipulating an interplay of physical contours that are also expressing limits, capacities, and values.

generation of designers who believe they have the power

IF YOU

Believe

IN YOUR SELF

Anything

IS POSSIBLE

To be *promethean*, just like the Greek semi-god who brought fire to mankind, means to be rebelliously innovative and creative. Simultaneously aligning a divine power for changing reality with creativity, the figure of Prometheus seems perfect to frame how a certain critical discourse on design envisions the discipline as an all-powerful force that designers can wield upon the world, just like the Original Flame.

Designers can take hold of, dismantle, and rewire some of the abusive structures of Capital by manipulating an interplay of physical contours that are also expressing limits, capacities, and values.

Keller Easterling
On Political Temperament (2021)

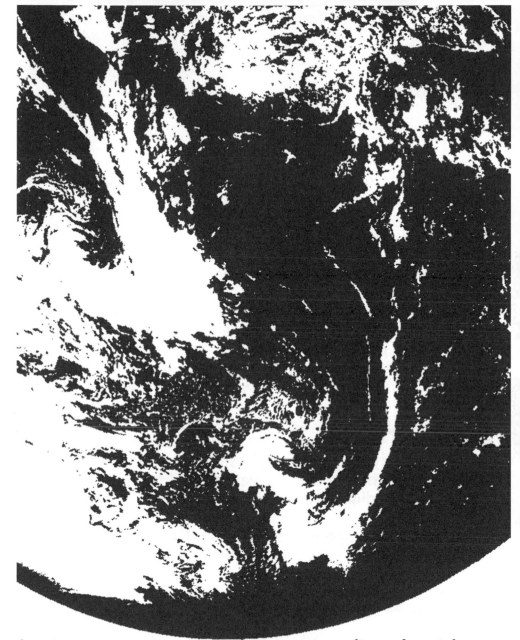

Designers are now urged to engage directly with the megamachine, the hyperobject, the Stack... with Capital itself. This novel synoptic view resists synopsis: it doesn't show, like in the past, the illusion of an orderly terrain, but a stormy sky heaving on a frightened practitioner.

Silvio Lorusso
No Problem: Design School as Promise (2020)

31

A.
"THE SUBJECT SUPPOSED TO RECYCLE"
as explained by Mark Fisher

originally published
by Zer0 Books

2009

Late cultural theorist Mark Fisher, in his 2009 book *Capitalist Realism*, references the paper *The Subject Supposed to Recycle* by Campbell Jones to exemplify how, under neoliberal capitalism, individuals end up being responsibilized individually for phenomena that pertain to the mechanics of complex systems and structures. Structures are not people — they cannot exercise responsibility, so they recede into invisibility by offloading such responsibility into our hands. But as individuals, what can we do? When there's no collective subject, what can we do alone?

In posing the question, 'who is the subject supposed to recycle?' Jones denaturalizes an imperative that is now so taken for granted that resisting it seems senseless, never mind unethical.

Everyone is supposed to recycle;
!!!!
no-one, whatever their political persuasion, ought to resist this injunction. The demand that we recycle is precisely posited as a *pre-* or *post-*ideological imperative; in other words, it is positioned in precisely the space where ideology always does its work. ;)

But the subject supposed to recycle, Jones argued, presupposed the structure not supposed to recycle: in making recycling the responsibility of 'everyone', structure contracts out its responsibility to consumers, by itself receding into invisibility. o_o

Now, when the appeal to individual ethical responsibility has never been more clamorous - in her book *Frames Of War*, Judith Butler uses the term 'responsibilization' to refer to this phenomenon - it is necessary to wager instead on structure at its most totalizing.

Instead of saying that everyone - i.e. *every one* - is responsible for climate change, we all have to do our bit, it would be better to say that *no-one* is, and that's the very problem. >_<

The cause of eco-catastrophe is an impersonal structure which, even though it is capable of producing all manner of effects, is precisely not a subject capable of exercising responsibility. The required subject - a collective subject - does not exist, yet the crisis, like all the other global crises we're now facing, demands that it be constructed. :/

B.
WHAT WE CAN'T DO
Afonso Matos

Similarly to the *"everyone is supposed to recycle"* discourse, the *"power of design"* discourse contracts out responsibility onto individual designers. On the one hand, it aims to show to the outside world the relevance of design in hopes that society at large will recognize it. But on the other hand, it is usually a narrative which circulates within "the bubble," in books written by designers and consumed by designers. It is then not necessarily raising the world's awareness about design. Rather, it strikes *us*, and it does so with double effect: it inflates our egos and fuels our hubris, while simultaneously setting the bar extremely high for the tasks that should be occupying us, in sharp contrast with the daily jobs which pay our bills. We should be, as Lorusso writes, engaging *"directly with the megamachine, the hyperobject, the Stack... with Capital itself."*[1] Anything less than that is an avoidance of the responsibility that our supposed power entails.

[1] Lorusso, S. (2020, December 7). *No Problem: Design School as Promise.* Entreprecariat. Retrieved November 26, 2021, from https://networkcultures.org/entreprecariat/no-problem-design/

But to talk about power isn't the same as talking about agency. Agency relates to the capacity of a given agent to exert its influence and make free choices in relation to a structure which constrains them. Borrowing these concepts from sociology is helpful to then understand that designers operate within a system which chains them to multiple forces — to a structure. So, design as a world-encompassing system might be powerful, but when we talk about designers as individuals, we should rather discuss not their *power* but their *agency*: given certain constraints, what can they actually do? Maybe not that much. This distinction between the power of design and the power of designers is put forward by Lorusso in his research about *Design and Power* for the Other Worlds online magazine.[2]

[2] Lorusso, S. (2021). *Design and Power - Part 1.* in Other Worlds #4.

To illustrate this stance, he brings the example of the Gillette razor, as discussed by dutch philosopher Koert van Mensvoort:

> *Obviously many designers and engineers have been involved in the creation of many razors over the years. [...] but what more are these creators of the individual models than little cogs in the perpetuating Gillette Company? Calling them engineers and designers is arguably too much credit for the work they do, as they merely sketch the next razor model, of which one can already predict the 'innovative' new properties [...] It's not like they are in a position to think deeply on the meaning and origins of shaving, in order to reinvent this ancient ritual. Like bees in a beehive their work is determined by the logic of the larger structure.* [3]

[3] van Mensvoort, K., and Jan Grievink, H. (2015). *Next Nature: Nature Changes Along With Us.* Barcelona: Actar.

This brings us to the notion of Ontological Design[4]. Lorusso cleverly remarks how the Ontological Design discourse seems to imply that there is an equal relationship between creator and object, expressed by formulations like *"the world we design, designs us back."*[5] However, this is not necessarily true, because even though this suggests that we are as active in the designing of our environment as we are designed by it, *"the environment's capacity to 'design' us is stronger than the one that we, as individuals, have to design it."*[6]

[4] Ontological Design posits that the human condition is inseparable from design itself. It signifies "a double movement — we design our world, while our world acts back on us and designs us." (Anne-Marie Willis, *Ontological Designing*)

[5] Laranjo, F. (2017). *Design as criticism: methods for a critical graphic design practice.* PhD thesis, University of the Arts London. pp. 20.

[6] Lorusso, S. (2021). *Design and Power - Part 1.* in Other Worlds #4.

While this seems complex, this ontological constraint is also related to a very palpable matter: designers are, presently, a tool of the industry. They are workers providing services, and thus they must respond to the demands of their bosses, employers or clients. That is their environment, to which they must abide if they want to survive. They don't have the capacity to change that environment (to "design" it), as much as that environment has the capacity to "design" them. Designers are usually *"too low in the power structure"*[7] to bring any kind of change into our realities through their intentions. Such intentions very rarely align with being in a position of authority where they can hold a grip upon most of the decisions that are made.

[7] Ibid

The dream of Critical Design is, then, to counter this lack of power, propagating the image of a designer whose role concentrates all roles (creating content, editing, designing and producing) — an independent author(ity) divorced from the demands of the market. But in what contexts can this image hold ground?

C.
MEETINGS TRANSCRIPTS

The excerpts below are extracted from the 3rd and 4th meetings, where conversations about the agency of designers and our complicity with capitalism may give us interesting insights into the kind of attitudes we take towards the discipline: should we resign design as a profession because it's complicit with the current system? Then, what other jobs are there left that don't participate in it? Can we just resign to work altogether? Can we move beyond individual responsibilization (*"I will decide to not design anymore"*) and into collective action? What really is our responsibility as designers?

MEETING NO.3 — 31/03/2022 — 17h30-19h00

A.M.
I'm reminded of this example, this book called *Radical Indigenism*. There was a full uproar about it on this architecture meme page, @dank.lloyd.wright. The book advertises or showcases indigenous technologies and how they could be productive to take into consideration for the design and architecture field, going beyond just *sustainable design*, into what has been called *regenerative design*. However, in the end the person who wrote it is basically behind a Masters programme that has ties to luxury good industries.

T.C.
Yeah, it's something that I find hypocritical. But hypocrisy is everywhere.

We are embodying hypocrisy.

We are talking about regenerative practices, we're talking about liberating the code, free internet, collaborative stuff, but at the end, what are we doing here? Don't you feel this? Every morning I'm like: Wait, I did a project about local economies and not buying food...but then, I did the project, I did the performance, and after that I'm going to Lidl, to Albert Heijn, to buy my groceries. There's a moment, I don't know when, when we're going to say: *Ok, my design practice and my personal life — I have to mix them.*

A.M.
...Or go the total opposite way around and say: *let's not mix them altogether because they are from the get go incompatible.*

Because being a designer is... just a job.
I.P.
T.P.
But maybe first you do this project and then it starts taking more and more place in your everyday life, and then step by step it ends up changing your own way of living. And I think it can have consequences and become proof of something — you show that a different way of doing things is possible. And by doing those things by yourself, it's also more powerful. A design project could only be about your own life.

^ meme by
@ethicaldesign69
(FKA @neuroticarseb…

G.D.A

But then you are kind of an outsider in the field of design. And if we consider how precarious it is, then being able to do this depends on your background. Maybe I have a bit of a different opinion from those who work in the field of information and publication, but with a background in industrial design, what you can do is just to *stop doing design*. And then, picking on what T.P. was saying about starting to change the way you live along with the projects you do, doing it more locally, I agree with this — but I also wonder: then how are we gonna do it, in a practical way? I worry that sometimes it sounds nice but it's really hard to do in practice.

T.C.

Big question: How are we going to pay our rent? Do we really wanna pay our rent? Do we want to maintain these class privileges? Or do we want to leave them behind? Because, sure, if we want to maintain them, we need a job, and we need this system, and all that. But if we rethink these class privileges, we can rethink all these other things. But that means maybe putting effort into stepping into an uncomfortable zone.

S.G.

[to A.M.] I don't know your intentions from the beginning of this project. But I could take it that, in a way, you started this because at a given point you wanted to do Critical Design *and* get paid for it. And then you realized that you cannot have both.

P.L.

But you can practice design as just a job and then have a critical, political practice in other ways.

It doesn't have to be connected to design.

T.P.

I don't agree.

I.P.

[adding to P.L.] ...And your personal identity affects your job, and your job influences your identity in a way. So, they always merge because it's your job in the end, and it's part of you, but in the end I don't think that you have to sacrifice your life for design. It's a bit extreme.

T.C.

What do you mean, sacrifice your life?

I.P.

You can be critical anyway and be conscious of what you do without design itself being an integral part of your identity.

A.M.

I think what I.P. is saying is — and of course it's not the same thing — but imagine a person that's working in McDonalds. Both that person and a designer in some random corporate design agency, they're both workers. Would you judge the McDonalds employee saying something like *"How can you work for McDonalds?"* like you would judge a designer asking *"How could you work for that corporate studio?"*

T.P.

When you're a designer, there's a responsibility. You're really helping the machine continue. But if you're working at McDonalds, maybe you're supporting the system a bit but not in the same way as when you're doing design. And about sacrificing things, I really see design as a tool that you can use to get to a point, but what matters is that that point is not design. It's not design for the sake of design, not an end in itself. So you're not sacrificing yourself by doing design, you're just using this tool you've learnt. And there are many other tools that we can use for many other purposes.

and now we jump into...
MEETING NO.4 — 07/04/2022 — 18h00-19h30
because this same conversation also then picked up again...

(...)

I.P.

I think believing that you can only enact change through design...that's when we start looking down on other people or other professions. Saying that "we can be political because we're designers," and saying that these people that have other jobs are not political in their profession, which is not true. I think your political beliefs, your identity, is always entangled with your work, but still that doesn't mean that it's *dependent* on your work.

J.D.

But I think it becomes problematic when your design work is something that goes against your political beliefs. What if the company that you're working for is super problematic or you have to actively ignore your own political beliefs in order to be able to work on this project? I guess that's where I would see the problem.

Y.B.A.

But this is where I think it is important to make a distinction between what is systemic and what is moral or ethical here. Because making this decision will be ethical to you. But when we're talking about racism and so on, they're systemic questions. I feel like we have a tendency to take systemic questions and moralize them. And when you moralize them, it gets hard because we start individualizing them. And I think, to some extent in our life, we will always be confronted to do this kind of things...

...and what does it mean if I have to take a job in McDonalds as a cashier to just live?

V.S.

Exactly, that's what we were saying last time. The bottom line is the same. If you're doing critical design, but you have to work for Thuiszbezgord to be able to afford to be in school and have this kind of practice, it's kind of the same thing as me, probably, doing pamphlets for Rabobank, and having a nonethical output in that job, but then doing other types of activism or other type of community work or something like that. You're just inverting it but the bottom line is kind of the same, I think. So basically...

...I don't think I have more agency as a junior designer designing a booklet for Rabobank than I do delivering burgers.

I think it's the same type of agency, or lack of agency. But! But: I can have a different type of agency in both those jobs, whether as a junior designer in Rabobank or delivering burgers, which is that I can make sure that me and my colleagues aren't exploited in the workplace, try to organize with them to ensure that the company doesn't have practices which are racist or misogynistic or sexist, etc. Because I have that labor link with which I can organize with other people. And it doesn't necessarily connect that much with the practice in itself. It mostly connects with the fact that I'm a worker.

and back to...
MEETING NO.3 — 31/03/2022 — 17h30-19h00

I.P.

And imagine the person working at McDonalds. They might be really concerned about the same societal issues that we are as designers, but that person doesn't have enough money to study design. Isn't that person not able to do the same with their lives, in political terms, without the "tools of design", as you want to do as a designer?

P.L.

Also you have to eat. And even though you're thinking about all these issues as a designer, not all designers can have an impact. For example, if you are in a certain position, you can take a decision that maybe for you is considered ethical. Like, "okay, I'm in a very high position in this studio. I can control the clients that I'm working with, and so I can have some impact." But outside of that bubble, to put that pressure on top of you, saying to yourself "okay, how can I, in my practice, be ethical towards myself and towards the world?", is something very complicated because you still have to pay to eat, to live. And you can do your best but...

T.C.

For me, we are already thinking in a very capitalistic frame of mind.

Saying that we have to pay to eat.

meme by
@ethicaldesign69
(FKA @neuroticarsehole)

V.S.

But you can't just really escape it, T.C. In the short term, I don't think it's realistic. I know that it might sound like a very reactionary thing to say, that it's not realistic. But at the same time, once you have that economic pressure, when you're facing that financial cliff in front of you, it's not like you have many options, I think.

T.C.

I think there are ways to escape this. An embodied and sincere practice that doesn't allow us to think about eating in the way that we are eating, paying rent in the way we are paying rent. There are already community models that are working and they have freed themselves from all these issues.

P.L.

With design, as a profession?

T.C.

Design as a profession? No, design as a profession — it's bullshit.

P.L.

But that's the question, like, I can just leave design. But the question is: how can you, through design as an ethical practice, change your perception of eating, of paying rent? Even if you can, how?

I.P.

Like, design has its roots in capitalism...

T.C.

But that's because we're still considering design as a profession.

BUT I WOULD PROPOSE TO FREE OURSELVES FROM WORK.

T.P.

Working means getting money from someone else to pay for your needs. If you consider yourself as a designer, you consider design as work. But if you free yourself from work, then design…

I.P.

But how would you do it? Now? From our position right now? How do I stop working? Because I want to! I really want to. [laughs]

P.L.

HOW DO YOU FREE YOURSELF FROM THE CONSTRAINTS OF CAPITALISM?

T.C.

We go to Emmaus, you know Emmaus? This place where people are getting trash from other people and capitalizing from it in order to live in community and cook together and live together, because they are marginalized people? Because the people that aren't there are not marginalized, they fit in the norm, they fit in the pre-established way of living. But people who are marginalized, because they don't fit, they have the agency to reinvent new models of living. So I would go to Emmaus and get with them. I'm pretty sure there's loads of communities that are working in this way.

S.G.
But then... I don't think you'd be renouncing design.

T.C.
For sure, I don't think I will leave design as a tool, but I will leave design as a profession. Because it depends on what we mean by design. There's some things we should put aside and some others we keep. And doing things that are built in a community, in a collective context, for me it's sincere.

AL.M.
To me, I would ask myself, is it worth leaving design as a profession? If you, as an individual, leave it, it's fine, it's your own decision. But it's something that, in the time you will live in, it will continue existing. So do we want to be part of that and try to change it from within? I'm not saying that putting a critical perspective into the field will solve every issue there is. But still, maybe trying to incorporate this perspective instead of, like, completely...

G.D.A.
You mean, subverting from the inside?

AL.M.
Yes.

V.S.
I mean this is a conversation that is a century old already, do you reform or do you revolutionize? What is viable? What is more desirable? It's a very long discussion and it has been ongoing...

AL.M.
Because I recognize both choices. Both are valid... Because I think it's just a different way of trying to be radical. I don't think there is just one way. Because still, if you decide to refuse everything, of course you'll be radical. But then I think it's also radical to kind of...

"stay with the trouble"

and, from within, recognize that this thing will exist, whether you like it or not, and that you cannot eradicate it alone. But I do recognize what you [T.C.] said, but I'm also questioning whether other alternatives are valid.

T.C.
It is not going to go away for sure...

A.M.
What T.C. is talking about, I think, is basically radical imagination. I think his point is basically that if we are already thinking within these pre-established structures and we're not actually challenging the very reality of work, then it can box us inside that same way of thinking. At the same time, right now there is no way- I mean, it's not that there is no way! There are ways. I don't wanna sound like Margaret Thatcher and say that there is no alternative to capitalism! What I want to say is that it sometimes becomes a matter of individual responsibility, which is also, still,

very much part of the neoliberal cultural common sense, in which we say "*Ok, I'm going to take this ethical position and leave design as a profession and go to a commune*" but in the end this will be an individual decision that you make. The real challenge seems to be that there is no way to create a collective subjectivity. There's only individual subjectivities right now.

I.P.

That's why unions work from the inside. If you have many people thinking about the same thing, so you build that collectivity from there...

V.S.

Yeah and they work for many issues. Not just labor rights.

AL.M.

[to T.C.] That discomfort you were talking about — I also feel it very much. But I wouldn't feel so sincere and legitimate leaving everything, you know? Because this is the context I grew up in. And I do realize that we're extremely privileged. So knowing that I come from that position, I wonder: how can I act within this context to change it in some way? Maybe it's just a transition towards some radical change in the future. But somebody needs to start preparing the ground. And I think that if you don't see it as a transition and you directly aim for complete day and night, it's difficult to really achieve something.

T.C.

Totally agree with what you say. It's about embodying what we are, sincerely. And that's something that is new and we still don't know how to do it, and we cannot define it yet. I don't know if we can gather together, if we are strong enough to try and stay together, to go deep into what we want to do. I don't know, but I'm super excited to work on it.

D.
SYSTEMIC CHANGE!
Afonso Matos

As design dematerialized into an attitude, it became a mode of engaging with the world — in other words, a politics. By becoming an attitude, rather than just a mere profession, Design ends up incorporating our public and political identities as well. This is very clear when we look at the hubristic gaze that the discourse employs. This god's-eye view, a souvenir from Modernism, materializes today in claims that design and designers can engage in "systemic change." Designer and researcher Dan Hill argues for such a thing in his book *Dark Matter and Trojan Horses: A Strategic Design Vocabulary* (2012). The synopsis reads: "*Strategic design is about applying the principles of traditional design to 'big picture' systemic challenges.*"[1] Of course, the discussion around systemic political change is necessary today more than ever. But it is also important to understand how such pressure is offloaded onto the individual designer, as we've seen before with *The Subject Supposed to Recycle* exam-

[1] Hill, D. (2012). *Dark Matter and Trojan Horses: A Strategic Design Vocabulary*. Strelka Press.

43

ple Mark Fisher brought us. Who is the designer who is in place to do such a thing as systemic change? Who is the designer that can sit at the table among the upper echelons of power? When does *authority* (decision-making, reserved for those at the top, who decide what is to be made) coincide with *practical execution* (the work of those who are at the bottom, the tools, the designers)?

Hill extends this thinking to neoliberalism itself:

> *We can even think of the ideologies at play at any time as being a result of, or a manifestation of, design decisions. The dominant market-oriented neoliberal hegemony across much of western society, for instance, had to be actively inculcated.* [2]

[2] Ibid.

While this might be true, the scale of design Hill talks about here is very far away from the scale of design we are usually engaged in — this "we" including both the service designer doing packaging labels or the critical designer doing a research project on deep sea mining at Het Nieuwe Instituut. Even if we train our systemic thinking (and that is, for sure, one of the biggest qualities that critical design education brings) our idea of action is still predicated on individuality. We should *"practice design at the level of systems,"*[3] but each to their own devices, each with their own individual practice: It is *my* design practice, *my* project, that will help subvert these dynamics. *"Exactly how, no one ever manages to explain."*[4]

[3] Laranjo, F. (2020, September 24). *Graphic Design Systems, and the Systems of Graphic Design.* in *Modes of Criticism 5.* Eindhoven: Onomatopee.

[4] Poynor, R. (1999). *First Things First Revisited.* Emigre. Retrieved November 24, 2021, from https://www.emigre.com/Essays/Magazine/FirstThingsFirstRevisited

Another famous example of "designing at the level of systems," which has been the object of scrutiny in social media, is architect and Yale professor Keller Easterling's book *Medium Design.* In an article promoting the new book, the author argues that *"designers can take hold of, dismantle, and rewire some of the abusive structures of capital."*[5] Easterling also jumps on the bandwagon to assert that *"everyone is a designer"* not necessarily of objects but of environments. She argues that we all design our way out of undesirable situations in our daily life. Her bold claim is that this design methodology can also be applied to political struggles. This can be done *"by*

[5] Easterling, K. (2021, January 18). *On Political Temperament.* The Double Negative.

manipulating an interplay of physical contours that are also expressing limits, capacities, and values."[6] because *"space embodies so many undeclared potentials that can reduce violence and create value through new arrangements – none of which need to go out of their way to exacerbate the violence of a political fight."*[7] The abstraction of Easterling's writing isn't relieved even when she gives practical examples, for example when she calls activist Rosa Parks a designer by saying that she *"activated an undeclared urban disposition, and she shifted this potential in the spatio-political matrix to break a loop without intensifying a dangerous binary."*[8]

[6] Ibid

[7] Ibid.

[8] Easterling, K. (2021). *Medium Design: Knowing How to Work on the World.* Verso. pp.135-136.

Writer and designer R. A. Hawley critiques Easterling's medium design while also linking it to *design thinking.* Hawley writes: *"where design thinking is primarily focused on process, Easterling appears interested in design as a kind of political theory — or rather, a theory by which 'design' transcends politics, rendering it obsolete."*[9] Easterling tries to present Medium Design as a salve against the outdated notions of ideology or activism, which only seem to breed violence. Those are not cool, not sophisticated. Design is. So, political struggles are now to be solved through design. Hawley is very direct when they argue that *"perhaps it's most helpful to think of medium design and design thinking as (...) one larger design-as-politics worldview — one that is willfully ignorant and fundamentally centrist."*[10]

[9] Hawley, R. A. (2021, March 25). *Middle Management.* Real Life.

[10] Ibid.

Design-as-politics implies that it is through design itself that political change can be achieved, because design transcends politics — like a God who can act from above. But history has reminded us, time and time again, from William Morris to the (subversive-turned-mainstream) postmodernist design experiments of the 90s, that as much as design tries to escape capitalism and subvert it *by itself,* wanting to bring about any kind of productive change, it ends up failing and being subsumed into it. Perhaps it is society itself which needs to change, and only then can maybe a different design exist, a design *otherwise.* I'm not sure that it is a different design that will bring about a different society.

Framing design as art or as an ontological life force is all fun and games until you have to pay your rent
:/

3.
FRAMING DESIGN AS ART OR AS AN ONTOLOGICAL LIFE FORCE IS ALL FUN AND GAMES UNTIL YOU HAVE TO PAY YOUR RENT :/

On the nature of design (As a profession? Or as more than that?)

This chapter concerns the complex position designers occupy today in terms of their relation to labor. Design seems to have dematerialised from a profession grounded in the mastering of specific technical skills into more of an *attitude*, a way of engaging with the world. Through that lens, design is not just a profession, but rather a sort of life force that exists within every human (and non-human) being. So, everyone can be a designer. Whether that is true or false is a bit beyond the scope of this chapter. This section, instead, wants to focus more upon *how* and *why* we got into such a state of affairs. Why are some designers now trying to position themselves more as research-ers and intellectuals? Why do we devalue technical profficiency as a lowly affair? And what are the *implications* of this shift for how we conceive our own horizons of po-litical action? Why do we think of ourselves more as creatives which can act upon the world through our design practices, rather than as workers which don't have that much agency when working under someone's orders? Departing from the case study of graphic design, but also with intersections from the field of architecture, this chap-ter contains materials that aim to explore the roots and consequences of the "designer as author" and "designer as researcher" ethos that schools like DAE seem to purport.

INDEX

A.
MEETINGS TRANSCRIPTS
p. 48

B.
6 THESES ON THE
DEPROFESSIONALIZATION
OF DESIGN
Silvio Lorusso
p. 55

C.
TYPOGRAPHY, AUTOMATION
AND THE DIVISION OF LABOR
(EXCERPTS)
J. Dakota Brown
p. 57

D.
IF "LABOR IS ENTITLED TO ALL IT
CREATES", WHERE DOES THAT
LEAVE GRAPHIC DESIGN?
(EXCERPTS)
Interview by Somnath Bhatt with
Jack Henrie Fisher, Alan Smart, Greg
Mihalko and Danielle Aubert
p. 60

E.
NOT EVERYTHING IS
'ARCHITECTURE'
(EXCERPTS)
Marianela D'Aprile
p. 63

A.
MEETINGS TRANSCRIPTS

The transcripts below are taken mostly from the 1st and 3rd meetings, where we can read interesting insights regarding the relationship of designers with labor and craft, as well as two different positions on the nature of design: one worldview which perceives design just as a profession, as merely work, and another which sees it as something more than that, as a kind of life-force embedded in all human beings.

MEETING NO.1 — 10/02/2022 — 17h30-19h00

V.S.

We're trying to clean up the street without having our own house cleaned up.

The state of the design labor market at the moment, or the labor conditions we have to subject ourselves to, are pretty bad. They're financially precarious...not sure if they're economically precarious? Maybe they are? Kind of struggling with that definition as well...But if you don't have that type of economical, financial safety in your life that you should have as a worker, that all workers should have, that's something that undermines so many aspects of your life — I mean, how are you going to this type of work that is going to enact some kind of critical change? How are you going to fix the world if you're not doing anything at all to address your own conditions?

M.B.

I have a question for you [A.M.], which echoes the question I had after the meeting we had with Beatriz Colomina. What pushed you to define the question you presented us with, *"Who can afford criticality?"* because now I feel like the conversation is evolving towards the idea that *criticality equals precarity*. But if you look in the field, autonomous designers, whether they're critical or not, are in a shitty precarious situation.

THERE'S NO INSURANCE, NO RETIREMENT, NO STABLE INCOME.

So it feels to me that this question of criticality is not necessarily connected to precariousness or to affordability. Perhaps the question lies somewhere else, on what we talked about, on *"What can criticality afford?"*, on what can you provide, to the field, to the practice, through a critical practice? But I'm afraid we might make risky parallels and risky assumptions if we continue in that other direction.

A.M.

Yes, I recognize that, but I think this question was more of a starting point, more of a provocative stance. I ask *"Who can afford to be critical?"* in the sense that there is clearly a type of design done inside a set of institutions that forgets to check in with the reality of work beyond those institutions. So the link doesn't go as deep as saying that *criticality equals precariousness*. It goes to the point of saying that, in these contexts, criticality *'forgets'* to consider precariousness as one component of it. We many times consider many other dimensions of oppression, as we should, because if we're addressing any dimension of oppression, it should always be at the intersection of all other dimensions of oppression, but we might forget to think how we are going to behave as workers beyond this institution. How are we going to enact this change, to continue addressing all these dimensions of oppression, beyond the context of being in a bubble, in a school that allows us to do it? So it's indeed more about the precariousness we face as any type of designer, critical or non critical, service designers or critical designers.

(...)

V.S.

It's more because what financial precarity does or economic precarity does is that it is a form of oppression that affects almost everybody in the world at the moment. What you see is a worsening of labor and economic conditions all around for anybody who works. And I think that that's something that we need to take into account as well. It's also part of that intersectionality. It's race, it's gender, sexuality, but it's also economics, finance, class, I think.

Because the thing is: the university is a great space for people to get together and discuss things that they have in common and maybe enact something from there. But, for example, especially in the last century, many people would also have other other spaces or other common causes that could help them get together to also think about things and take collective action, which was the very profession that they had. And by all of them identifying with one profession they would gather around and form unions, organize strikes, organize whatever it was to enact some positive changes to them and to other people around them that probably also weren't in their profession.

(...)

M.O.

I also have the feeling that being a designer is almost like an identity.

Other people, like my friends who do Computer Science, they don't feel like they're computer scientists, they don't put that in their bio. Whereas I feel like, being a designer, it's like it's part of our identity. It's very hyperindividualistic at times. You're trying to create your own brand. It's almost like a reflection of who you are.

A.M.

And we feel that we need to brand ourselves in a certain way to survive in the very competitive field that is design. So, we describe our practices as being at the intersection of art, technology and science and politics and also ceramics... [laughs] And sometimes, "at the intersection of all those things, the only person you find is you." (paraphrasing Lorusso). So you're at this intersection and someone's at the other intersection and you can't build bridges or solidarity, because sometimes you might both call yourself designers, but you have practices that are completely different. How are you going to even discuss the terms under which your work happens? What are the common things that bring us together? I think it's an interesting question. And when we're so concerned about trying to distance ourselves from each other, to appear marketable to the outside world, we may be forgetting that it could be nice to just say "I'm just a designer, a graphic designer, and that's okay." I shouldn't need to call myself anything more than that. I don't know, I think there's some power in that humbleness. We should ask ourselves where this need for differentiation comes from.

49

AL.M.
Also, because design practice is expanding, which is exciting, but also
diluting more and more, at the same time, which is slightly dangerous...

V.S.
And I think that's also where you could almost start to make an argument
that defends that perhaps we should be more like technical workers. That,
you know, perhaps we should act as citizens and act as workers, and not try
to imbue citizenship into the design work itself. Because if you just do
technical work, but you organize with other people who do the same type of
technical work and you gather together with them and you say: "*We're going
to boycott doing work for like, BP Oil*" or against some kind of company that
enacts practices that aren't good — there's also a lot of power in that.

We shouldn't shy away from defining ourselves as "mere" technical workers.

, because the power of enacting some change can come from defining that kind
of common ground. Instead of doing a design piece that critiques the action
of that company, you could actually, once you have the base for it, try to
organize with others...

I.P.
—Not that trying to have a critical practice is wrong...You can achieve a
lot of things if you do critical pieces on those things. It's just that it
won't give you any financial security. And you need to get that somehow. And
for me, I've always had part-time jobs, because design jobs never paid for
my needs. So it feels like you have a double life because, like, you're at
school, and you're very critical and very intellectual... And then at five
you go work for a restaurant. It feels like...

your personality is completely split.

MEETING NO.3 — 31/03/2022 — 17h30-19h00

S.G.

There's this woman in Colombia that is very successful at organizing people
and she stopped the deviation of a river. And she's doing these actions that
have real impact in real communities.

And she's doing it not through design, but through means of organizing people, gathering people together.

I.P.

You could call it design in this school and people would eat it up. [laughs]

A.K

But that *is* Social Design in a way. To get people together. Or also

when you choose to work in a certain workplace. And from where I look at
it, it's also a way of just looking at your own life and enjoying it in a
way. When you dedicate your life to the public in a certain respect. Then
the impact comes from there….

S.G.

No, what I'm saying is that she doesn't describe herself as a designer.
She's a politician, a social leader.

A.K.

We might call them social leaders, we might call them public figures, whatever. But they are performing social change, they are driving some sort of
difference. So for me, when I look at it, it is a social design practice.
But again, as we said, we don't know what social design means, because it
means many things. It doesn't mean only one, so it's very difficult to define
something and that's why we always have different views. And we know how
to define a surgeon because a surgeon performs a surgery. But we don't know
about the social designers, who think about people in general, just because
everybody has their own definition of it. So what you're saying about the
woman who's doing effective work in Colombia....I think they are design
practitioners, too. They're using tools, they know people, they know behav-
ior. They have an understanding of how people might drive change. We try to
learn the same thing. So I think it's very similar, but in this setup it's
very difficult to do.

I.P.

So every worker that, through their work, provokes social change, is a designer?

So for example, a doctor can also be a designer or a politician is also a
designer?

T.P.

It depends on if you consider design as a discipline or design as a tool,
as a way of engaging with life...so...

yeah, everybody is a designer.

51

A.K.

For me it's like: we make things work that most people think of. People think many things, but they don't make it happen. I think the only thing which we do is that we make it happen. We can get out and we make it. That's what differentiates us.

A.M.

I think this highlights two different perspectives on design. One, is that we see design as this innate human force, a human drive that everyone has. Everyone has the capacity to make decisions. You just decide one thing instead of the other, and thus it's a design choice because you're taking one action and influencing your surroundings in one way and not another. So for example, I can say that I'm designing this group, I'm designing this meeting. But you could just say that I'm organizing it. So it's a linguistic question — but I think here linguistics are important to take into account. On the other hand, I think we have a notion of design that is tied to the socioeconomic constraints under which we exist right now, which is the fact that for 200 years, with the Industrial Revolution, design came to be known as a discipline, and as a set of professions, that is connected to the making of things. Designers started making things. And we are under a certain economic paradigm that ties design with capitalist profit. Now, I think it's super interesting to think of design as an innate human life force that everyone has inside of them, and the idea that everyone can be a designer. But I also don't think we should forget the fact that we are bound, as designers who are professionals, by certain socioeconomic constraints that we can't just leave altogether completely. And in that sense, I would agree with you saying that that organizer, that Colombian activist, could be a designer, if I were to completely disregard all these constraints that we have. But at this moment in time, in these circles where this type of discourse circulates,

I think calling that person a designer or social designer actually benefits more these elite design spheres and not so much the person or the activity that such person is pushing forward.

I think that benefits more the discourse on design that capitalizes on actually colonizing other disciplines by saying "*oh, they're also doing design and design is this and design is that.*" And by *saying* that, through linguistics, they're legitimizing design further and trying to show to the world that design is essential because it can drive social change. But in the end it's just appropriating the traditions of other human activities and ways of engaging with the world. Saying that design is all these different things, I don't know... — well, it actually might be! It actually might be. But in this current context, I think it's actually feeding a certain elite, because it's saying that those who partake in these kinds of designing are more social, more politically concerned, than the "lowly" technical designers that are just doing, I don't know, corporate logos or something like that.

A.K.

I come from a handicraft background. And when I sit with a portrait artist, or with a weaver, that equates me to them. And in their work they combine their heads, their hands and their heart together. That's what design for me is. Sometimes you don't have a head, or heart, but you still do things with your hands. And the skills that they perform — I don't have those skills sometimes. Maybe I have the academic skills, or the worldwide experience. But I think what equates our practices is that they bring their head, hands and heart together to make something. And this is a balance that we don't have. We suffer because we don't have these three things aligned together. Because it implies compromises. It's beautiful how craftspeople work in every indigenous community. And these techniques, they're so specific sometimes, they're part of their traditions, their family heritage. So it remains inside their family. But they perform it with a certain degree of sophistication which we're still trying to learn. They've had it since ages. That's why I learn from them and that's why I'm now here learning more things from a different perspective.

S.G.

But I think that the case of an artisan is different from the social worker example, and I think that's my point. You see that social worker trying to benefit social communities as a designer, but I see that statement more as design trying to become some sort of pseudo social science instead of accepting that it's a discipline tied to materiality, to craft, and that it's technical. And then if we accept that we're just technical workers, we can get to become more of a craftsperson, in which we accept our material conditions and techniques and try to imbue that sort of technique with sophistication, instead of trying to make design some kind of pseudoscience, which we're not even taught to do. Like, this school hasn't even taught me anything about sociology, or whatever theory, or how to aid certain communities, or how to do anything. Because,

I don't think this school knows what it wants to be.

A.K.

But regarding that idea of a pseudo social science...I mean, from where I read it...for instance, we've been reading about Buckminster Fuller. He came up with the design of a geodesic dome. He named it as the first geodesic design, but in India, in Gujarat, which is a state which is all desert, the communities used to have houses made of mud which were round, just because they would have better ventilation and cooling systems. But when Buckminster Fuller visited India, and saw that some people were making round houses, instead of the Western geometric houses, he came up with his idea and only after was it given the name of geodesic design. It all started long before any ascription of "design." Before, it was not design. It was just a part of their tradition, their process of doing things. For me, it started long ago.

P.B.

I heard once that design means actually to designate. And that the first designer was a primate that used a stick. And before the design profession came about, there were *grafistas* (graphic artists), *delineantes* (drafters), and they weren't called designers. And at some point the word design appeared and then now we have this conflict...

V.S.

I think this whole linguistic discussion can drive us away from the notion of design as a profession.

, and designers as professionals, as craftspeople in a way. And it's eroding that type of class solidarity or labor solidarity that you can have in
other professions. You know, you have engineers unions, doctors unions, you
have carpenters unions. And we don't have designers unions for some reason
because it all became so sparse.

S.S.

We're just too fragmented. If I don't take a job, you take it, etc...

V.S.

But that's the thing. This whole linguistic conundrum, of "*everybody can be
a designer*" or calling design to all these different things, it's eroding
that type of notion. You were saying something before about complimenting
the craftsmanship of an artisan by calling it design. I don't think that
we need to call it design to elevate it. It's already elevated in its own
right. What he's doing is maybe already more valuable than what our notion
of design is.

A.K.

Yeah, no, no, that was not the intention. I'm not in a position to compli-
ment them. They are on a higher scale of expertise.

V.S.

But yeah, I think the bottom line is...that's the discussion we should be
having and it's cool to think of design as a tool and all that, but I think
we should think about design as a profession.

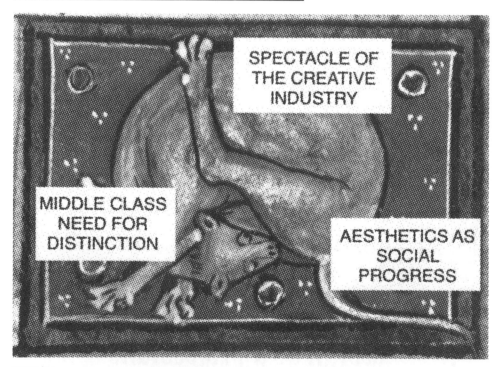

SPECTACLE OF
THE CREATIVE
INDUSTRY

MIDDLE CLASS
NEED FOR
DISTINCTION

AESTHETICS AS
SOCIAL
PROGRESS

meme by
@ethicaldesign69 (FKA @neuroticarsehole)

B.
6 THESES ON THE DEPROFESSIONALIZATION OF DESIGN
Silvio Lorusso

Taking the cue from the previous page, where one of our participants commented that "*we should think about design as a profession*", this short collection of arguments by Silvio Lorusso tackles exactly the issue of deprofessionalization in design. This process of deprofessionalization can be seen in the ubiquity of calls for democratizing design and in statements like "*everybody is a designer.*" Weaving a critique of this deprofessionalization is not about gatekeeping the profession. Rather, it is about understanding why it is happening and what consequences it has on designers.

published in Entreprecariat

November 3, 2021

1.
According to Donald Schön, a professional is someone who "claims extraordinary knowledge in matters of human importance, getting in return extraordinary rights and privileges." This definition proves that a profession is necessarily exclusive. Claiming inclusivity by calling for a complete deprofessionalization of design is mere populism.

2.
The current calls for design deprofessionalization legitimately denounce how the design profession has disproportionately excluded marginalized groups. However, they ignore the mechanisms of deprofessionalization that affect the design field in the first place. This is a problem, because higher education—which is where these calls generally come from—is bound to generate resentment and anger if it cannot guarantee to its student body, which invests time and money in its institutions, the social and economical benefits of the profession. >:(

3.
In the context of design, extraordinary knowledge is expert knowledge. We need to ask: how much of this

expert knowledge does the designer actually hold in the public perception? If the designers' knowledge is not considered, at least partly, a form of expertise, they won't be granted the status of professionals in the social arena.
:(

4.
In the eyes of the general public, certain design sub-fields such as graphic design do not possess any "esoteric" knowledge. The perception is that thanks to the common availability of digital tools and devices, everyone can design a logo or a book. For several people the fact that there are MAs in graphic design is a source of astonishment. :0

5.
Whether this perception is right or wrong is irrelevant, as it does and will nonetheless shape the economic relationships between clients and designers, and therefore the social status of the latter. The effects are already apparent in the salary gap between specialists in UX design, which is still considered an esoteric practice, and those in graphic design, which is fully demystified. :/

6.
Some designers recognize that there is no fundamental difference between their supposedly expert knowledge and that of a profane. Instead of trying to convince the public of something they don't even believe in

themselves, they attempt to regain the benefits of a professional position (prestige, credibility, higher income) by placing their expertise within the domain of cultural production, i.e. by presenting themselves as intellectuals. Thus, cultural production is not just the casual ambition of some aspiring intellectuals, but the result of their field's failure to generate or maintain the impression of expert knowledge. Ironically, the very calls for deprofessionalization belong to this process.
>_>

C.
TYPOGRAPHY, AUTOMATION AND THE DIVISION OF LABOR – A BRIEF HISTORY (EXCERPTS)
J. Dakota Brown

originally published by Other Forms

Chicago, 2019

The acceleration of this process of deprofessionalization, in graphic design, can be associated with the ubiquity of certain digital tools and softwares. The way these technological advacments influence the socioeconomic status of workers is also the object of study of J. Dakota Brown. Brown analyses, in the following text, the legacy of journeyman printers, drawing parallels between their struggles (with the automation of their trade throughout the 20th century) and the ones that graphic designers face today (regarding the "demystification" of their profession, as Lorusso remarks).

As critical historians from Karl Marx to Henry Braverman and David Noble have shown, the progress of capitalism's division of labor entails a gradual transfer of control and planning from the factory floor to management.

The growing coherence and confidence of the graphic design profession is accompanied historically by the gradual fragmentation and decline of the printing trades.

The job description of "printing" originally encompassed a set of knowledges that extended far beyond the point of contact between ink and paper. Early printers were often also type-founders, publishers, and booksellers.

Print workers thus held a strategic position in the circulation of public discourse, which was simply not possible without them.

In the 1970s, print production involved a complex hierarchy of work processes, the final product of which was never fully visible until it had been printed. Designers could only approximate typographical treatments; directions on spacing, size, and weight were then handed off to phototypesetting shops to interpret in detail. A separate group of prepress specialists followed designers' directions on variables like color density and image placement, and then "stripped" together disparate negatives to create a print-ready master. But despite the many hands through which such work passed, much of the period's modernist-influenced design left the impression that it was the product a singular, detached mind.

Though there was still a high degree of churn in new machines and processes, this division of labor held stable until the arrival of Apple's Macintosh computer in 1984. The personal computer centralized capacities formerly bound up in massive metal-founding operations, delicate apparatuses of type on film, or astronomically expensive, room-filling computers—to say nothing of the highly specialized workers that attended these machines, or of the systems of education and apprenticeship that such a workforce presupposed.

By the mid-1980s, typographical technology had reached a height of modernized seamlessness which, ironically, contributed to the decline of modernism's hegemony in graphic design. New design software facilitated effects like layering and distortion, which were quickly put to use in visual polemics against modernist clarity.

By the 1990s, the postmodernist critique of modern rationality and power had grown more rigorous. However, the movement's theorists showed little interest in grasping capitalism as a determining context for their theory and practice; transformations in the political economy of print were thus largely ignored.

The postmodernists' focus on cultural intervention often neglected the material contingencies of the practice. Semiotic theory and cultural studies opened vistas to broad contexts of symbolic circulation, but often at the cost of such bare facts as design's own relationship to waged work.

Capitalist technological development has rendered texts and images almost infinitely reproducible—and has built unfathomable electro-libraries in the process. But despite this gigantic aggregation of productive force, it is still necessary to put people to work moving words and pictures around, most often in the service of brand competition among otherwise identical commodities. What confronts us is not a world in which machines have freed people from work, but one of mass unemployment, in which some of the most celebrated "innovations" are apps that facilitate short-term, low-wage, benefit-less contracts.

If graphic designers became typesetters, they may turn out to be the last typesetters. The design software that repackaged the knowledge and skill of the printing trades seemed at first to deliver a dreamed-of autonomy to graphic design as a profession. But because these technologies were off-the-shelf consumer products, trained and credentialed designers have less and less of a monopoly on the medium. A general facility with image and text has bled into general literacy—due in no small part to the ease of pirating such "immaterial" commodities as Photoshop. In the contemporary design press, articles on apps like TaskRabbit and Fiverr, or a future role for AI in the automation of design decisions, recall the mix of anxiety and reassurance that characterized coverage of the Linotype nearly 130 years ago. These projected "disruptions" may well turn out to be empty hype. But whatever is in store for graphic design in the coming decades, it will be impossible to understand without accounting for the capitalist constraints and imperatives that have shaped the practice from the beginning.

meme by
@ethicaldesign69 (FKA @neuroticarsehole)

D.
IF "LABOR IS ENTITLED TO ALL IT CREATES",
WHERE DOES THAT LEAVE GRAPHIC DESIGN? (EXCERPTS)
Interview by Somnath Bhatt with
Jack Henrie Fisher, Alan Smart, Greg Mihalko and Danielle Aubert

Following from Dakota Brown's analysis, Somnath Bhatt interviewed designers who
have been discussing the relationship between designers and labor, asking *"What does
a labor-centric design practice look like?"*

originally published
by AIGA Eye on
Design

May 13, 2021

One of the most enlightening, empowering, and transformative experiences I had
as a design fellow at the Walker Art Center was organizing last March with my colleagues and comrades to form the Walker Worker Union. Now over a year later, as
I freelance away, waiting for my stimmy to drop, with no health insurance and an
even more uncertain future ahead, I often contemplate what kinds of political and
structural agencies and forms of coalition are available to graphic designers today.

Specifically, I've been thinking a lot about the slogan, *"Labor is entitled to all it creates!"* This slogan comes from the Ricardian socialist thought that states that labor
is the source of all wealth and exchange value. How would you apply this slogan to
graphic design, a service profession largely defined by the client-designer relationship, in which designers create something to hand over to someone else to generate
profit with. What, then, is the labor entitled to in graphic design?

How does our class position actually structure and limit our abilities to demand more
for our labor? What does a labor-centric design practice look like? What can we learn
from graphic design, printing, or typography history, and who are the people working today who can provide examples to how socialism can be practiced within the
design community? To get answers for some of these questions I sat down with Danielle Aubert, graphic designer and author of *The Detroit Printing Co-op: The Politics
of the Joy of Printing*; Jack Henrie Fisher and Alan Smart, designers, researchers and
co-founders of the publishing practice Other Forms; and Greg Mihalko designer and
founder of the co-operative design studio Partner & Partners. We spoke about how
they work toward expanding and deepening the criss-crossing paths of graphic design and labor organizing—Solidarity Forever!

*All four of you engage in labor move-
ments and leftist ideology with your design practices. How did that come to be?*

Danielle Aubert

Graphic designers are the ultimate pre-
cariat, we're just these free floating agents.
A few years ago, I started researching The
Detroit Printing Co-op and got pretty
close with Lorraine Perlman, who was
one of the founders. They were IWW
members, and [the Co-op] has this slogan: "*Abolish the wage system, abolish
the state.*" I was in the archives and just
feeling like there was a lot of resonance
between what they were doing between

1969 and 1972 and the present contemporary moment. When Trump came into
power, I felt like I couldn't just hang out
in the archives anymore. I was radicalized
by reading a lot of the stuff that Fredy
Perlman wrote and learning about the
structure [of the Co-op]. You do start to
wonder, what's your role? What can you
do as a graphic designer? What do you
do as a person? I just started to learn a lot
more about political organizing.

Jack Henrie Fisher
Alan and I were also in New York during Occupy Wall Street. We had been in
a Marxist-Lacanian reading group in the
Netherlands. The first thing that Alan

60

and I produced together as Other Forms was a book related to squatting. The people who I considered my design peers in New York were totally different from the people who were my comrades, my ideological peers, and this was confusing. In general there's confusion about the political agency and class position of the professional designer, because there are different genealogies of that. On the one hand we can trace our professional origins to printers who were often politically radical members of working class movements. On the other hand, we clearly come out of management, whose job it is to discipline the working class. To interrogate how our class position actually structures and limits our political agency, we started a reading group recently with some other graphic designers who are both curious and confused about what kind of political agencies are available to graphic designers.

How have your politics affected the way you run your practices organizationally?

Alan Smart

There are important distinctions between the way you actually work, what your work is about, and who you do that work for and under what terms. You can be working for Pentagram as an on-the-books, salaried designer, but you're working on a coffee table book on radical movements of the 1960s, or you could be an anarchist collective that does ads for Nike.

The Ricardian quote "*Labor must own all it creates*" makes me think that in the U.S. and in the world at large there's this as-yet unresolved effort going on to figure out how class works right now. There's this curious interest in the 19th century Romantic way to look at pre-industrial forms of "free labor," which wasn't serfs or peasants but wasn't yet wage labor either. We are living in this awkward class position as architects, and designers, of being an independent freelancer, freeholder yeoman journeyman that is very much Petit Bourgeois. This is celebrated and valorized, both in the current neoliberal cultural discourse, and historically in the U.S. where there has always been a resistance to even admitting that there is a working class here at all.

How do you understand the role of power, autonomy and ownership in graphic design? What are some of the power dynamics contemporary graphic design unconsciously perpetuates?

Aubert

I was just elected president of our union at Wayne State and there's a clear admin, there's the dean, there's the provost, the board of governors who are on the other side. And that's where you come up against power. But when you're a freelancer, you end up having 85 bosses. There's no one locus of power I can withhold my labor from to assert autonomy.

Greg Mihalko

It all comes down to, who's paying for the work we do? If we are supplying these services or forms to a client, it implies that there's some demander demanding that this work needs to be done. Who has power and who reproduces that power? Who has the capital to pay for this stuff to happen? What do we do as laborers to challenge that or pervert that in a way to gain more autonomy and power?

How do design history and labor history criss-cross?

Aubert

Design history and labor criss-cross with printing. The International Typographical Union was a major labor union, and one of the first unions to admit women—but it is also important to remember that they were conservative. There's anecdotes of them in Detroit, blocking the printing of the black power newspaper Inner City Voice. J. Dakota Brown, who's done a lot of research on the International Typographical Union, has made arguments about the field of graphic design's transition in the '80s. There's a few key things that happened: In 1983, Philip Meggs' History of Graphic Design was published, which gives some solidity to the field. Then in '84 Apple IIE comes out and you get advanced graphical interface capabilities. In '86, ITU dissolved. Typesetters and old relationships to labor go away and then all that work becomes the purview of the graphic designer, who's doing it all on a computer. Labor becomes immaterial and abstract.

Fisher

The contemporary graphic designer's relationship to historic labor is sort of fuzzy. The antecedent is not exactly the kind of printer-laborer who was in the ITU. In many cases the "designer" was inaugurated as a profession in order to break deadlocks between management and labor.

For example, formerly, ITU worker-printers controlled the point of production. If they went on strike, newspapers couldn't be printed, nothing could be printed. So the workers had tremendous power over things that produce knowledge. They had a kind of strategic importance and power that we no longer have. Does a position like this—control over the point of production—exist in contemporary design media? It doesn't seem to...

Mihalko

What that means in my opinion is that the graphic designer is the last thing that's considered. Like, "Oh, we've got to get a graphic designer to put this all stuff together. How much money do we have? Well, we don't have that much money at all, but let's just find someone that can do it quickly and not pay them a lot."

Aubert

Problem is that if you don't do it, they'll just find someone else.

Smart

Designers are screwed from the get go.

Similarly, architects in a Western sense were invented as a category in the Renaissance as an effort to break the power of the stonemasons guilds. So the role of the architect or a designer was this kind of bourgeois intellectual who is not a master mason but still holds a lot of power and decisions.

How can graphic design be more receptive to alternative models of ownership and class-consciousness?

Mihalko

Design schools and design publications should present it more as a valid alternative and not a rarefied, exception to the rule. We also shouldn't be talking about the work that other major studios produce as the best examples of design right now. If you continue to prop up these examples of design—how they were produced and who they're produced for—it has an effect on how and what people think is possible. We've been conditioned by education and publications and awards to hold up versions of design or types of design that don't consider class or social value.

Fisher

An important way is to actually understand how complicit graphic designers are intuitively with the interests of capital. Polemically within the discipline, there are a lot of narratives that get espoused about the capacity of graphic design to make social change. To imagine graphic design itself as actually outside of the class struggle is a flawed position. Just remembering how conditioned design is by its subordinate position in relation to capital is really important.

What are your thoughts on the gig economy and its effects on design labor?

Smart

The gig economy as an idea is a part of this larger liberal effort to get rid of the industrial labor model. We should be thinking about the way it offloads the cost of production onto the workers who are trying to escape the industrial labor model, and how they then "escape" into this even worse or even more fraudulent other thing. There's a promise of: "*You're free. You're an independent worker.*" I am like, "*Am I actually? No, I'm not, I want health care and I want to be sure I get paid.*"

Aubert

We've been doing gig economy type stuff since we've had our own computers. Boots Riley often gives this example of the longshoremen on the West Coast being a really hard group to organize in the 1930s. People were like, "*You can't organize them as laborers because they're all independent,*" but then they were organized and now they're a really strong union. I think about that with graphic designers. Can you organize graphic designers as a group? I think it's hard but, you know, people out there are trying to organize the gig economy workers.

Someone in the DSA gave me this advice: organize at work, start with where you work [if you're working in-house]. I've been in touch with a lot of people who are trying to form a union. It's hard but

it's a good move to start to do that. If you're freelancing, decide to not exploit other people's labor. Simply don't hire unpaid interns or make people work for exposure.

Fisher

I remember seeing a work presentation that Richard Hollis gave in the Netherlands. Something that was remarkable to me about Richard was that as he was talking about projects and about his graphic design and rehearsing some anecdotes, his political commitments just naturally, almost accidentally, showed through. He worked with different unions and for Pluto Press, and there was a definite left wing theme in the content of his work then. This was in contrast to some of the other graphic design presentations we saw that day in which certain Dutch designers ended up theorizing their own practice of graphic design as something with this inherent agency that could intervene in larger political issues, that the form of their design had a sort of political agency. Whereas with Hollis, the political commitment was something separate. He just happened to be left-wing, his graphic design didn't give him special political powers.

E.
NOT EVERYTHING IS 'ARCHITECTURE' (EXCERPTS)
Marianela D'Aprile

In the previous chapter, we discussed architect and researcher Keller Easterling's statement of how designers "*can take hold of, dismantle and rewire some of the abusive structures of capitalism.*" Journalist Marianela D'Aprile reacts to Easterling's theorizations arguing that they have consequences for how architects perceive themselves more as powerful, radical agents of change rather than as technical workers that are dependent on someone else to pay for their labor, and thus are constrained by such relationship. Easterling's book *Medium Design* can be seen as one more instance of the phenomenon of deprofessionalization Lorusso talks about.

originally published by Common Edge

January 26, 2021

Architecture theory most of the time has little consequence on the politics and machinations of the world. Thus Easterling can get away with not making sense because, who cares? But, there are real, insidious consequences of this mode of engaging with the world and with politics through architecture theory. It's been

taught in architecture schools for so long that it has created hordes of architects who enter the workforce indoctrinated into thinking that just because they look at the world with some kind of critical eye, they are radicals. That they are above and beyond politics, that they can opt out of reality—which is full of struggle between two classes of people, those who have to sell their labor to survive and those who buy that labor—in favor of their projections of what the world is. In actuality, they cannot do this. They, like most people, are workers. They have to sell their labor, rarefied and mired in intellect as its form may be, to survive.

(...)

Easterling's work turns a purposeful blind eye to that. And, it posits that we can hack capitalism, make it slightly better, design our way out of it. This is nothing but an attempt to circumvent class conflict, which is the only thing—as striking teachers, nurses, longshoremen, and Teamsters have shown us in very recent history—that can bring about favorable change.

If, like I mentioned earlier, people who work in architecture do indeed feel a pressure to engage in this political moment but lack the vocabulary or framework for it, then they should learn. Architects and other professionals are taught to identify first and foremost with their job; it's a great tool of capitalism to alienate us from our lives and make us servile to nothing other than profit for someone else.

But all of our actions don't have to pass through the profession. We can engage with the world as people first—and as workers.

Get politics. Be clear about what they are. If you want people to listen to what you have to say, learn to write. If you're a centrist, say it. But quit trying to hack capitalism.

OK, I'LL BITE. HOW ARE ARCHITECTS SUPPOSED TO CHANGE THE WORLD WITH NO POWER AND WITHOUT PROLETARIAN UNITY WITH FELLOW BUILDING INDUSTRY PROFESSIONALS

meme by
@dank.lloyd.wright

OK
WHAT IF
DESIGNERS
UNIONIZED
?
....?
HÄHA
JK...
UNLESS...

4.
WHAT IF DESIGNERS UNIONIZED...?
HAHA JUST KIDDING... UNLESS......

On collective power.

This chapter concerns the material conditions of designers, money, labor, precarious-ness and also what we can do (together) about it. What collective agencies are available for designers today, beyond our individual practices? Critical Design seems to propose that if we are to act politically upon the world, then we must do so through our designing activity itself. But what are we, beyond being designers? What would happen if we were to rethink our role in society, beyond being powerful agents of social change and creative actors? The "*designer as worker*" (as opposed to the "*designer as author*") might find that political agency comes not necessarily from an ethical or critical practice (which not everyone can afford to have) but rather from organising with other workers (not necessarily just other designers) in order to build collective power. Collective struggle is rarely considered in the historical canon of our field. We individualize the problems we face in our workplaces instead of understanding that we can build bridges of solidarity from talking openly about them. Can we change this somehow?

INDEX

A.
MEETINGS TRANSCRIPTS
p. 68

B.
POLITICS BEYOND DESIGN
thesis excerpts by Afonso Matos
p. 74

C.
WHAT COULD A UNION DO
FOR GRAPHIC DESIGN?
mixed materials by Evening Class
p. 76

D.
ABOUT THE INTERNATIONAL
TYPOGRAPHICAL UNION
J. Dakota Brown
p. 78

A.
MEETINGS TRANSCRIPTS

The transcripts below are taken from the 3rd, 4th and 5th meetings. In the final meeting, the 5th, the conversation got more practical and grounded on sharing the lived experiences of DAE students with design work, internships and the struggles they have already faced within the design labor markert.

MEETING NO.3 — 31/03/2022 — 17h30-19h00

A.K.

Why do you think we don't have design unions?

V.S.

The path to becoming a professional designer is much different than in other professions, for example. And I'm not saying that that's a problem necessarily. But that's a contributing factor, for example. And the definition of design is also very broad, which also makes it harder. It's not like becoming a civil engineer where you have to take these steps and do these specific things, and everybody kind of correlates.

A.M.

Also in these kinds of critical design circles in which we are right now, I think it's very easy for us to fall more into idealism and forget the material constraints which we will face in a few months or are already facing in some cases. And it's great to have this kind of place to actually consider a more idealistic stance and what design is or how design might actually be something that existed even in the first hominid that used a stick or a rock to make fire, which is probably true if you think about it...But right now it's also a profession. It's also something that many people earn a living from. And those people are sometimes in very precarious conditions or working under unregulated conditions.

I.P.

Also have in mind that we are here and we pay to be here. And that money comes from somewhere. So we work to be able to pay this or our parents work for us to be able to pay thid. And are our parents' jobs as ethical as our view of design? I don't know. We have to think about where that money came from.

V.S.

We need to look at the world in a material way.

I.P.

Yeah. It's hard not to look into the world in a material way. We have so many constraints.

P.B.

I made a project about brick manufacturers. And when they started making unions, they would meet to talk about money. These meetings, maybe in the next steps, **they should be about money.**

How do you earn your money? How do we get money?

And so, taking this suggestion, the fifth meeting was mostly about sharing experiences about money and work. So we jump into
MEETING NO.5 — 18/05/2022 — 17h30-19h00

J.D.

I've worked for two months, project-based, properly paid as a designer after my Bachelor. I've done loads of internships, mostly unpaid, but these two months were properly paid. I got 2000 a month. And basically what I felt the entire time when I was working was like:

"Damn, am I really, worth these 2,000 euros that you're paying me?"

And even still now...I'm thinking like: *"Why am I even putting myself down so much?"*

H.K.

Once I had a job offer but the pay was not enough, so I couldn't accept it. So, I could either go for that and then have to work somewhere else at the same time or I could just ask for more money. And so I did the latter and somehow, there was more money! They weren't really expecting someone to ask for more...but then somehow they had it. And then I did the same thing for a freelance job. And it's always a scary moment because you never know how people react. But I think it's really important to just ask for the money you need and if they don't have that amount then you can lower down but it was interesting to see that somehow, if you ask, there might be money.

N.M.

It's always scary. I remember my first internship. I worked for £15 pounds a day there.. In England, it's actually illegal to do that, but design studios just don't give a damn. It was a very small studio. Then it went up to 25 and at the very end he asked me to write a review and and I said "I think it's not fair that you're paying people this small amount" — it was a cool studio but bad, bad pay — and he said to me, he sent me an e-mail saying "Well you should've just asked for more!" And I was like "F*ck you!" [laughs] But I was like 20. I was on my first design internship. So I think if it was now with more experience...yeah, I'm always going to ask for more now. But if you're just learning, if you're just a newbie, right out of design school... it can be scary. So this is why these conversations are important.

C.M.

I have a story from two weeks ago. A friend of mine who works for quite a big company asked me to do a freelance job, just a few things. So she asked how much I wanted for that and I had no idea how to budget it, because it was something that I had never done before. Basically she asked me to do two company profiles and one brand book which are like PDFs and that are very important actually for the company, they are presentations of what their philosophy is. So basically I had no idea of how to budget it. So I texted my former boss, where I did an internship, who is a person I have some proximity to, and I was like: "Hey, I got this offer. I have no idea what to do. Can you help me?" He answered:

"Hi. Great. Sincerely, I am not the right person to ask because my prices are out of the market. In my opinion, you should just start, as we all did, even if you try and fail many times."

69

and I was like...what kind of advice is that? Just try and see what happens? I don't see why you can't be more transparent. Even if you think you're out of the market you can say: "I would ask this, but I'm out of the market."

A.M.

How much did you ask in the end?

C.M.

So, one pdf came with an InDesign model that they could use. And I asked 500€ for that one and then I asked 700€ for each of the other two. So it's 1900€ in total. And I still have to pay taxes.

(...)

N.M.

I was thinking, after graduation, looking for a design job and some of us are thinking about moving to Rotterdam and trying to find a job there, and all the graduates I've spoken to, are like: "Wait until the graduation show" and I'm like "That's in October, I can't wait that long!" and they were like "Trust me, wait" and I was like "What do you mean?? [laughs] What's going to happen in October? Some kind of miracle?" But for me,

I just can't spend all summer not having any money coming in...

G.W.

I have a friend who worked as a graphic designer for KeyArt in Hollywood. And I mean, the entertainment industry is always well paid, but it's always really, really intense. And then in some cases they submit an idea but then this company actually commissioned multiple agencies to have ideas, and eventually they get these first drafts and then they don't pay them, they just pay the first drafts, and then they combine and have their own concept. And then usually they're super excited, like "Oh we have, for example, Stranger Things as our client." But then they only get to make the very first round of sketches...and then people just don't have passion to work on anything because nothing is really promising.

(...)

AL.M.

There's a whole universe of conversations that we can open in and around internships because they're supposedly not paying you in exchange for education, experience, exposure, but still they expect professional performance. So they're not really teaching you anything and they're also not paying you...so, there's a whole problem there. Because of course if you decide to do one, it means someone else is supporting you financially. You need to have some sort of capital. You make it as an investment...

J.D.

I did have one of those, and I could afford it because it was an erasmus internship...but the problem with that one in specific is that that specific studio always has 4 to 5 interns, and there's 2 bosses and 1 employee. So,

most of the time, there were actually more interns than actual employees, and they don't pay at all.

V.S.

Yeah, but some of those studios, like...the owners of the studios, especially when they're smaller, many times they're probably not also exactly like "fat cat" designers, it's not like they're riding around in their BMW and have a massive houses or anything. It's more that sometimes the market is so cutthroat and clients will just pay for the least that they can that these people end up having to resort to these very dishonest and very exploitative practices because that's the only way they have to compete. And that's also very toxic.

G.W.

Another thing maybe is how you define success with graphic designers... because as I said before, there's a huge gap between the pays, at least in the context I'm familiar with, and then there's also competition going on for designers...How do you define your success? By how much you get paid or by how many followers you have on Instagram? How able you are to create, like, cool-looking posters or whatever? But I feel like, at least in my previous experience,

there is always this invisible competition going on.

So it was this kind of taboo to talk about it, even how much you get paid because you do realize you get paid very differently from other people. So in a way, if people can start to realize that we are all the same and we're all exploited, and that there is no competition, and we are all concerned about just surviving, maybe we can then start talking about forming unions or having some sort of solidarity.

MEETING NO.3 — 31/03/2022 — 17h30-19h00

V.S.

Yeah, yeah. Because it starts with talking about living conditions, but then it also can evolve.

Once you have that collective organization which is more focused on labor rights, you can organize to do many other things.

P.G.

It starts with money. It starts with "How much are you getting?", "Can we share that resource?"

V.S.

Yes, it's a way of beginning to build that collective subjectivity that you [A.M.] were talking about.

L.T.

And also we need to start asking our teachers— I mean, I always try to ask all the teachers how much money they earn. How they get it. I was talking with this famours designer once and he told me he got paid 6000€ for the logo of a really big fashion brand. Which is not that much considering the brand we were talking about. The thing with the "money talk" is that...

...everyone feels uncomfortable.

And we shouldn't. We should share so we can see the standards.

I.P.

It's super weird because you don't talk about money in design. You talk about money everywhere else but here in DAE we're pretending we just don't make money. But people make money and it's just not discussed. It pushes us more apart from each other because we're afraid of this thing that's going on that we don't know how it works.

P.G.

And everyone says that it's not interesting to talk about money. But no, it's super interesting to me to talk about money. That's how we know the standards. So, everyone, let's ask our teachers, we need to know how much they charge.

T.C.

Can you define precarious?

A.M.

I think it's a way of living that is, first of all, temporarily and financially insecure. So you don't know for how long you're going to have how much money, or resources. You have these resources for now, but you don't know for how long. You're always in this constant anxiety of how can I assure that I have secure conditions for living.

T.C.

And the objective is to get out of precariousness?

A.M.

That's the thing. You could take that stance and say "let's stay with precariousness" because maybe it is by giving up on certain things that we can take on more of a radical role. But do you think that it is a necessary condition that we need to face some kind of precariousness in order to...

T.C.

I don't know, but with these gatherings, I would like to know where we are going, you know? If it's to gather to get out of precariousness and reach some stability and give to the profession of design some other status in society? What is the aim? Maybe we can define it together, but yeah.

I.P.

I also think that

following the stance of "staying with precariousness" really depends on your condition.

Like, can you even do it? Because imagine that you have a child or you have to care for your mother and pay for stuff for them? Would you be able to make that stance? Would you even have time to consider accepting economic precarity for the sake of a radical design practice? I think there's a lot of things that play into that.

AL.M.

Also being physically able to.

V.S.

You don't want to be homeless or hungry. You want to stay as comfortable as you can.

AL.M.

Also, like,
precariousness shouldn't be a long term plan.
We can accept it when we are young, able bodied, because when you can move freely around, you're much more flexible. But in the long run it's difficult to sustain, also mentally. So if we normalize precariousness, in the long run, for me, it feels dangerous.

T.C.
Yes, for sure, for sure. But what is precarious for you is maybe different from what is precarious for me.

H.K.
It will be different for everyone, a bit.

V.S.
I think the baseline is getting rid of that fear that, in a short amount of time, you can be left in a complicated position, having your livelihood in danger.

MEETING NO.4 — 07/04/2022 — 18h00-19h30

V.S.
Because money and your economic status are such a big part of the material conditions that make up how you're living. And now we've accepted that material conditions are such a big driver of what you can or cannot do. So I think it's something that you also need to take into account. I think that the place that we're coming from is that once you accept that you need to make money in order to live, in order to exist — from there, what agency can you have? Once you see you're stuck in there?

Y.B.A.
But then maybe we can start as a students. Even as a student, design costs money. And...

...NOW WE WILL BE ARRIVING AT A GRADUATION MOMENT WHERE YOU KNOW IT'S GOING TO COST MONEY.

And who's able to afford something grand while another person can't? So money is shaping your project. Some people have 1k, 2k to invest while others don't even have 100€... I feel like just acknowledging that between ourselves is important to not end up in an individualistic competition about who has the better stuff. But we need to ground it back to: what are we part of? And I feel like what we're trying to do here is to build up a community, bring us together as a community. And when you were talking about the printers in the 40s or 50s, I think what worked is that thet had dependancy — these people were dependent on each other. And because you are dependent on someone, you create social relationships from there. And this is maybe what's important here: how do we create dependencies between ourselves? In terms of skills, of resources... But in the long run as well, and we were talking about positionality, and I'm from La Réunion — I'm going back to La Réunion afterwards. So...what do we do afterwards? How do we reconnect? To be honest, I've been in Eindhoven for two years, but I don't know any Dutch people, I have no sense of community here, except for Design Academy. And that's how uprooted I am from this place, as well. And that's why I'm craving to ask: what brings us together? And how do we push that? I think starting as students first makes sense. We all decided to come here. We're here.

73

B.
POLITICS BEYOND DESIGN
Afonso Matos

If we learn to identify not primarily as designers, in the sense of individual creatives who are in charge of putting forward their world-shaping visions, but as workers, who are bound by many constraints, we might find that through admitting this individual weakness, we can find collective strength.

We don't have to be political *through* our work, if we can't afford to do so. But this doesn't mean that we can't be political *about* our work — quite the contrary. Please note that this doesn't necessarily negate the idea that all design is an ideological process, informed by one's personal values, and can never be neutral. I still believe that politics reside inevitably in what we do as designers. However, I don't believe it is through this individual practice of design that we will be capable of bringing some sort of change to our present conditions. Design, by itself, will not trample systemic racism, patriarchy and misogyny or deeply ingrained homophobia. It will not stop climate change, or undo the modern/colonial matrix of power, or destroy the nature/culture divide. It will not undo the epistemological heritage of the Enlightenment nor the consequences of the Industrial Revolution. It won't hold the ruling class accountable. It won't hack Capitalism.

Instead of letting the urgency of enacting systemic change paralyse us, we could maybe try to have a positive impact in other, more local and humble ways. As my friend Serra says, "*we could first clean our own house before we try to clean the street.*" If we understand that we can be political agents outside of design, we can then learn about how politics work beyond it, how a major social structure constrains us — how we're precarious, atomized, individualistic, competitive professionals — and ponder upon whether collective forms of action could benefit us. Can designers ever unionize? Who is this us? How do we define a collective?

A few recent initiatives have worked on imagining forms of collective agency for designers. UK-based collective Evening Class, founded in 2016, started researching unionizing and made their findings public in an event they held in 2018, called *What could a union do for Graphic Design?* They intended to "*identify the*

1 Evening Class (2018, June 14). *What could a union do for Graphic Design?* Retrieved December 29, 2021 from https://evening-class.org/posts/what-could-a-union-do-for-graphic-design

2 Drumm, P. (2018, July 6). *This is What Starting a Design "Union" Looks Like.* Eye on Design. Retrieved January 12, 2022, from https://eyeondesign.aiga.org/this-is-what-starting-a-design-union-looks-like/

3 Ibid.

4 Ibid.

intersectional aspects of different forms of creative employment, in order to form an active community able to hold employers to account."[1] They researched other unions, both current and past, as well as co-ops, and arrived at the conclusion that *"the structures of specialized trade or craft-based unions don't provide the best blueprint for a designers union today."*[2] As such, they researched contemporary grassroots unions that targeted the ever-changing conditions of the gig economy and aimed to represent workers from platforms such as Uber and Deliveroo.

The organizers also found out how expensive and complex it is to build a union from scratch. One of the designers behind the initiative, Christopher Lacy, said that *"it's almost like setting up an institution: you need money, certain affiliations, political clout."*[3] Even so, their whole research led to a fruitful conclusion. Instead of starting a whole new union, they managed to set up a branch for Designers and Creative Workers inside of an already existing union, the UVW (United Voices of the World). The UVW is *"part of a new crop of grassroots, "bottom-up" organizations that aren't sector-specific, that are set up to respond quickly to issues that arise, and that tend to represent gig economy and nontraditional jobs."*[4]

DESIGNERS + CULTURAL WORKERS

Cultural work *is* work! Our Designers + Cultural Workers Sector is organising workers across the creative industries.

C.
WHAT COULD A UNION DO FOR GRAPHIC DESIGN?
materials by Evening Class

These materials were shared during the event held by Evening Class in 2018. They are screenshots from the presentation pdfs. The event was divided as follows:

19.00—Arrival
19.30—Introduction
19.45—Concerning Crisis: The Elephants in the Studio
20.00—Discussion: Who's the boss?
20.15—A Potted History of Some Unions
20.30—Discussion: What can we learn from the past to inform a response to our current labour conditions?
20.45—Solutions, or, things we could do collectively or individually

The following materials are taken mostly from the "Concerning Crisis" presentation, where the collective outlined the many problematics that graphic designers face when it comes to their working conditions and work culture.

NO CLEAR PICTURE OF THE INDUSTRY

We know problems exist from:
• Personal experience
• Talking to friends/colleagues
• Articles/News
• Campaigns (direct action)
• Survey/questionnaire
• Report (government or other)
• Workers' Inquiry

DO WE NEED A WORKERS' INQUIRY?

What is it?

At its most rudimentary level, workers' inquiry was to be the empirical study of workers, a commonly neglected object of investigation at the time.

What is* the aim?

To witness & frame problems experienced by workers as social & structural as opposed to personal & individual

LACK OF EMPLOYER RESPONSIBILITY

• Do you have a contract?
• If you have a concern/issue how do you raise this, and to whom?
• Do you know your rights?*
• How are you paid?
• Do they have an intern policy?

* 49% of business owners know the legal rights of interns.
38% of interns know the legal rights of interns
— Graphic Designers Surveyed (2015)

HOW WE TALK ABOUT DESIGN(ING)

• Situating design (like art) outside the realm of work
> Depoliticises the industry/practice
• Any political focus external, rarely internal (design solving global issues)
• Constant comparisons/analogies to other disciplines.
• Creativity framed as sustainable resource; live and breathe (and eat...)
• General culture of overwork
> Fatigue as evidence of success
• Discourse focused on end product(s)
• Designer Plus____ (designer-as-designer)

SIGNIFIERS OF SUCCESS ARE SKEWED

• Design blog post/feature
• Talking at a conference
• Teaching
• Publishing your own journal
• Re-publishing an old designers work, or an old companies brand guidelines
• A monograph; inserting yourself into the canon

So how do we turn the focus back on ourselves and our industry but avoid the designer-as-celebrity framework?

How do we reposition the graphic design as worker/producer?

And in an industry where personalised everything is encouraged, and competition is rampant, how do we transcend individualising our concerns?

HIGH EXPECTATIONS OF WORKER

- Exceptional command of all software (past/current/future)
- Self-promotion/social media presence
- Undergraduate (+postgraduate+) degree
- ___ Years of experience
- Multi-disciplinary
- Hyper flexible
- Outstanding, versatile, dense portfolio
- Excellent written and verbal communication skills
- (Demonstrable) Passion
- Ability to 'Think beyond the logo'

LOW EXPECTATIONS OF EMPLOYER

- . . .

'CREATIVE' WORK IS WORK

- Answering emails
- Liaising with clients/meetings
- Liaising with/sourcing suppliers
- Finding clients/Pitching
- Networking
- Studying/Project research
- Budgeting/Scheduling
- Keeping up with contemporary design
- Writing proposals/applications
- Designing

= Sitting in front of a computer for long periods of time

A CULTURE OF OVERWORK

- Unpaid overtime
- Long hours
- Free pitching/speculative work
- Short or non existent breaks (taken at your desk)
- Unreasonable or impossible deadlines/project timelines

WORK IS UNFAIRLY DISTRIBUTED

- Monopolies of certain types of work/client (cultural sector, publishing, regeneration projects, teaching etc)
- Over production/unequal distribution of projects
- Emphasis/celebration/focus on pro-bono/self-initiated work (autonomy)
- The yes men > who facilitates the yes?
- Culture of competition
- Undercutting
- Who is setting up practices?
- Lack of funding/paid interesting work

ISSUES OF REPRESENTATION
Gender Race Class

Almost every occupational sector has an underrepresentation of women in its workforce, with Publishing* (52.9%) and Museums, galleries and libraries (64.8%) the only two sectors where women are not under-represented compared to the workforce overall.
— Panic! (2018)

* ...over a third of the workers from the upper middle class social origins and only about an eighth from working class origins.

ISSUES OF REPRESENTATION
Gender Race Class

88% of those surveyed identified as 'white'
— Graphic Designers Surveyed (2015)

4.8% BAME workers in music, performing and visual arts
— Panic! (2018)

WORK IS UNFAIRLY DISTRIBUTED

Meritocracy(?) or Social reproduction(?)
- Talent
- Ambition
- Hard work
- Network* (who you know)
- Family
- Background and wealth (education: yours and your families)
- Gender and ethnicity

77

D.
ABOUT THE INTERNATIONAL TYPOGRAPHICAL UNION (EXCERPTS)
J. Dakota Brown

One of the unions that Evening Class researched during their investigation was the International Typographical Union, formed in 1852 to represent manual typesetters. J. Dakota Brown has written extensively about this union, and elaborates here on the kind of insights we first encountered briefly in the previous chapter (pp. 57—59). Studying the rise and decline of the ITU gives us important clues about the kind of political agency that was available to journeyman printers at the time, in sharp contrast to the lack of power graphic designers seem to have today over their own labor conditions.

Original publication:

Content by
J. Dakota Brown,
Ben Koditschek,
and Micahel
Neuchatz

Edited by
Chris Crawford,
Ben Koditschek,
and Jess Sattell

Printed by Platform

2021

The printed book was, if not the first, then certainly the clearest early example of the world of standardized, mass-produced commodities to come. The craft of printing was thus always linked to the doubleedged sword of mechanization: "labor-saving" innovations could render work less taxing and dangerous, but the primary motivation for their adoption was usually the reduction of labor costs— resulting in layoffs or slashed hours. Print workers often found themselves in the paradoxical position of fighting technologies that promised to ease the burden of their work. Rosemont offers the example of a more efficient ink roller, invented in 1814 and vigorously resisted by American printers. The existing standard was a more rudimentary instrument that required periodic soakings in animal urine to keep it from hardening. Printers worked in consistently squalid, poorly-ventilated shops that contributed to lower-than-average life expectancies.

Though Johannes Gutenberg's fifteenth-century press had scarcely changed in the intervening years, the first decades of the nineteenth century brought changes far beyond the humble roller. Innovations like iron construction and steam power fundamentally changed not only the shape of the machine, but the entire work process that fed and maintained it. With the industrial acceleration of presses, the process of setting type by hand became an exasperating production bottleneck. Several attempts were made to mechanize the process, with most ending in expensive failure.

In 1886 Ottmar Mergenthaler, a German engineer working under contract with the New York Tribune, presented his employer with the first successful attempt at mechanized typesetting. Like type composed by hand from a type-case, the Linotype machine utilized thin bits of metal, with the important difference that each such "matrix" carried the negative impression of a character. Seated at a large keyboard arranged by character frequency, the operator would type the matrices into a line. The space key inserted a metal wedge that could be used to uniformly expand word spacing, justifying the line at the touch of a lever. Molten metal was then injected into the matrices to form a full line in positive relief. Finished lines were stacked into columns and locked into page layouts for the press. Between each new line, meanwhile, the Linotype automatically re-sorted the matrices, replacing a painstaking job that had normally fallen to apprentices. While the Linotype was an expensive and somewhat risky investment, it delivered on promises of labor-cost savings, and in time it contributed to a dramatic enlargement of the size and circulation of the periodical press.

The International Typographical Union (ITU), which had been founded in 1852 to represent manual typesetters, was slow to appreciate the significance of machine composition. For a few years after the New York Tribune unveiled the Linotype in 1889, union newspapers often published reassuring reports on the poor quality of its output. A February 1891 article in the ITU newspaper Typographical Journal, for example, argued that the machines were "*overrated*," and little more than "*toys*" for print capitalists with no background in the trade. An article published the next month, however, summarized a report filed by union delegates after witnessing an "*improved*" Linotype in action. The delegates noted that the new design addressed earlier defects in typographical form, producing "*lines perfect in spacing and with a clear face*." At the same time, they pointed out the difficulties workers encountered in transitioning to a sharply accelerated work process with a complex ensemble of moving parts. The report cautioned against "*panic*," but acknowledged that far-reaching changes were looming, and closed by recommending that the union begin pushing for control over the new process.

In 1892, the New York Tribune and ITU Local #6 signed a contract that put the newspaper's machine composition under union jurisdiction. During the next decade, mechanized typesetting began to overtake hand composition, primarily in newspaper printing plants. While there was still a limited need for the manual composition of headlines, advertisements, and other display applications, the new work process soon touched off an employment crisis across the printing trades. Younger compositors scrambled to learn machine composition, while thousands of older or more narrowly-trained workers fell through the cracks. Those who could secure employment had assessments added to their dues, which provided thin relief to the unemployed. There were well-founded hopes that the expansion of print volume would eventually compensate for the loss of work, but it became a foregone conclusion that some number of unlucky men would be sacrificed to "*the latter-day wizard [of]* *Progress*" in the meantime.

The subsequent history of the ITU is thus a story of an organized trade coming to grips with sudden changes in the technical basis and organization of its labor process. Wherever possible, the ITU attempted to write developing technologies into its contracts. In some cases this involved outmaneuvering other printing trades, as with the lithographers; in other cases, unforeseen alliances were formed, as with Linotype machinists. The ITU also began to push for shorter workdays in order to claim a share in the benefits of the new technologies; redistributing the leftover working hours also kept layoffs to a minimum. As machine composition became the norm in the early decades of the twentieth century, the ITU tightened its grip on the Linotype, which helped it to grow into one of the most powerful unions in the country. However, the new century also brought a number of unexpected threats to the labor process built around the new machines. Mechanisms were developed to run Linotypes directly from telegraph tape, like a player piano; justifying typewriters with proportional characters threatened to turn secretaries into typesetters; and countless attempts at phototype-setting came and went, though these initially made more of a dent on display typography than running text.

In many cases, the development of these new technologies was explicitly spurred on by employers' desire to get around the union "problem." In 1947, for example, ITU Local #16 began a 22-month strike against six Chicago newspapers. In response, Chicago Tribune management ordered enough Varityper justifying keyboards to fill an office, and put its clerical staff to work typing columns for photographic reproduction. The "scab" paper had an uneven appearance and made some embarrassing missteps—including the infamous "Dewey Defeats Truman" headline of November 3, 1948—but it hinted at the possibility that a newspaper might someday be printed without the participation of union typesetters.

Linotype composition remained the norm at US newspapers through the mid-1960s, when the ITU began to make concessions on the use of computers and other technologies in exchange for large employer contributions to its *"automation funds."* But this time, the new machines did not simply change the printing process; increasingly, they dissolved typesetting into word processing. A centuries-old gap separating writing from printing began to narrow, and this was the very ground on which the ITU stood. Once more, the newspaper industry led the way in automation, and again the union scrambled to either train people in the new processes or encourage early retirements. The union suffered a long decline during the 1970s, and finally dissolved in 1986—which happened to be the centennial of the Linotype.

At the time of its demise, the ITU was the oldest union in the United States. Another way of putting all of this is to say that in the late twentieth century, organized labor's role in the history of typography came to an unceremonious end. Graphic design historians and journalists are often at pains to convincingly situate the practice in its social, political, and economic contexts. However, accounts of the discipline's history often treat the development of print technology as a separate issue—a politically neutral process of technical refinement. Philip Meggs' landmark textbook *A History of Graphic Design*, for example, offers only the briefest hints of the social dislocations that accompanied automation in the printing trades. One reads, for example, that the first steam press in England was printed in a secret location to guard against sabotage, or that vaguely-defined *"strikes and violence"* greeted the first American Linotype installations.

A side effect of downplaying the social constraints that shape the work designers do and the tools they use is a corresponding inflation of graphic design's agency in the world. In extreme cases, this leaves an impression of designers as semiotic magicians, unilaterally bending public consciousness to their will. This tendency is especially evident in the documentary *Helvetica* (2007), in which established practitioners and critics take turns arguing for a single typeface's role in the maintenance of ideologies as varied as socialism, democracy, Reaganomics, and fascism. In a segment that opens the film, the design critic Rick Poynor states that graphic designers define the very *"communications framework"* that mediates people's knowledge of the world: designers, he argues, *"are the people... putting their wires into our heads."*

(...)

At the dawn of the Linotype era, union printers protested the "monster" that had taken their place at the type-case: a machine that eerily replicated their movements without need for food or human dignity. If we stand in the shoes of these obsolete tradesmen, we can see modern design software from a different angle: as an accumulation of knowledge passed down through the "hands and minds," to quote Michael Neuschatz, of countless typesetters. This is a common refrain throughout the history of the ITU, and it was vividly rearticulated by the late Carl Schlesinger just as the Linotype was dying:

"Computers and cathode tubes replaced us, But, by God, they'll not erase us! 'Cause we taught them everything they know."

From a more familiar perspective, we might also observe that the typesetters' tasks were not simply automated out of existence; rather, many reappeared in the digital designer's expanded job description. The historiography of our field encourages us to see ourselves in a tradition of avant-garde painters, irreverent advertising professionals, and owners of well-heeled design consultancies. But thinking with the typesetters may permit us to acknowledge other realities: particularly those aspects of the job that are anonymous and repetitive. There is little in design history's parade of creative personalities that would prepare a student for the extreme expectations of flexibility and responsiveness—or the opaque pay structures—that define the life of a freelancer today. And a designer in an agency or studio may hear something unexpectedly familiar in Neuschatz's description of "patrimonial" workplaces, where a sense of obligation to the boss makes employment feel like a favor. Such readers will be interested to hear that union typesetters could once demand triple or quadruple pay for a late night of last minute revisions; that they had guaranteed high-quality healthcare; and that they had the option—when the need arose—to collectively withhold their labor and expertise, knowing that a broad network of mutual aid had their backs.

Trying to explain UNIONISING to these DESIGNERS be like...

Apes together strong.

meme by
@ethicaldesign69 (FKA @neuroticarsehole)

RESPONSIBILITY
BY THE EDITOR

BEING-IN

Throughout this research, I was constantly dealing with the fear that I could be perceived as trying to position myself as "better," more "aware" than my Critical Design peers, such as my colleagues from DAE, tutors, and other designers who work along similar lines. Ironically, this very dynamic is the one I was criticizing in the first place: those who brand themselves as "Critical Designers", "Social Designers", "Speculative Designers", "Designer Activists" and so on are positioning themselves as something superior to the "mere" Graphic Designers or Industrial Designers. This form of positioning is consumed not only by prospective clients and collaborators but also by peers, a way of signaling to the others that one also belongs to the same niche. This signaling is not necessarily (althought it could be) linked to any real concern or active work with the rooted, localized issues of real communities through a long-term engagement with them — it mainly serves to acquire cultural and social capital by *communicating* that one is concerned with such things.

This process has been called "leftwashing" by some, whereby one coats one's practice with a seemingly superficial concern with radical politics. More and more I see that this kind of criticism of "leftwashing", which is taken in part by this book, could be perceived as coming from a place of judgment, as if I'm taking a higher ground, looking down on the designers who do that. But I've done that myself in the past as well.[1] And the forces that were at play at the time, which instilled in me the need to do so, are still at play now for all of us: a need for differentiation that is fueled by an extremely individualistic and competitive field, where we're constantly comparing ourselves to our colleagues and their work — a landscape that is not "natural" or "as it is supposed to be", but was in fact prompted by certain political, socioeconomic and technological developments, as Lorusso and Brown have argued. Alas: not only have I done that in the past, I'm doing that *right now* with this book: "*clearly, no one is innocent, myself included: this very text is a positional product targeted at what is still a niche market.*"[2]

[1] My first bio, written in 2019, when I had just graduated from my bachelor, read: "*Searching for expanded notions of design through investigation; for new ways to activate social, political and institutional discourse; for utopian imaginaries and the possibilities they can materialize into reality; for both strategy and sentiment, handling hard and soft powers.*"

Do I know what I meant by that? No. Does it sound cool? Yes.

[2] Lorusso, S. (2018, January 19). *The Designer Without Qualities*. Entreprecariat. Retrieved September 17, 2022, from https://networkcultures. org/entreprecariat/the-designer-without-qualities/

But admitting to this embeddedness is perhaps how we break the danger of *being better than "x."* Otherwise, this project could be seen just as the next step regarding criticality in design, going from "Design" to "Critical Design", now to "Being Critical of Critical Design." That is not my purpose. Still, I know that is a risk I incur in. In fact: it's not so much that this book is *at risk* of being incorporated or co-opted into the Critical Design discourse, so much as *it is already part of it.* It will circulate within the same market, the same spheres, will be picked up by those who understand the lingo, the references, the memes, those who are familiar with the schools and the studios. Once, my tutor Simon, referring to the eventual appropriation my project could be subject to by the very institution I was critizing in the first place, said: "*whatever success your project has, that will be its own failure.*" I guess this better demonstrates that there is no escaping this state of *being-in.* Possibly that's also one part of what Donna Haraway talks about when she tells us to *stay with the trouble.*

This book, even if it has the intention to "critique criticality" (or rather, the social construction of criticality, not so much its objects), will still probably live inside the same bubble, the bubble of those who understand what Critical Design even *is* in the first place. I think that publicly assuming this can also be a powerful act, because then the intention becomes clear: it's about trying to make those of us inside the "bubble" aware of the bubble's own limits. It's about trying to get us to rethink why are we engaging with those discourses and what do we hope to come out of them.

GUILT

My friend Santiago once showed me this Timothy Morton quote:

> *There's nothing wrong with being a little bit hesitant and thoughtful and reflective. But anti-intellectualism is the favorite hobby of... the intellectual. At the end of ecology conferences, you so often hear someone saying, 'But what are we going to do?' And this has to do with guilt about sitting on chairs for a few days thinking and talking (and perhaps also with the sheer physical frustration of sitting on chairs for a few days).* [3]

[3] Morton, T. (2018). *Being Ecological.* Pelican.

This quote seemed tailor-made for my situation. There I was, being the anti-intellectual, making a project about the limits of this intellectualized bubble of design. That person at the end of the ecology conference asking *"But what are we going to do?"* was me. It's exactly what my internal voice sounded like, judging me during my Bachelor for "just" writing, researching and making "cool" Critical Design projects from the comfort of my laptop, while many couldn't afford not to truly engage in political fights, to be at the forefront of demonstrations, to riot, to strike. Meanwhile, I could just observe, write about it. I had that privilege. So, this internal voice brought me to this project — a project that partially comes from the positive drive of deconsctructing privileges (in myself and in others), but also from the very shadow of that drive: *guilt.*

But what are we going to do? is how I started the group meetings, because I wanted to take action instead of just sitting and thinking. I needed that catharsis, that absolution. *But what are we going to do?* is what we kept hearing as the meetings progressed and we couldn't bring ourselves to do anything. It started taking even a bigger toll on me because I saw quite clearly my inability to mobilize a group of people, and *to do something about it* (whatever *"it"* was). And maybe in the end I was in fact comfortable with such a thing — with just sitting and thinking. Still, I kept hearing this judging voice, setting me apart from myself and from others.

I started to sit with these feelings more and more throughout the year, understanding why I was doing this project in the first place. In my last days in Eindhoven, a friend and tutor for another Master at DAE, Gijs de Boer, asked me: "What if the real question is: Who can afford *not to be* critical?" This makes more sense than it seems: Most of us who inhabit these spheres and are engaged in these critical practices are doing it also because such positioning is what brings (*social,* which then translates to *economic*) value to our work amidst the process of deprofessionalization Lorusso talks about. In fact, many "Critical Designers" are precarious professionals, working at an exhausting pace, doing multiple gigs (and usually also teaching) at the same time. The only things setting them apart from "mere" designers being the way they construct their professional persona (often online), the kind of schools they went to, or the theories they were exposed to.

Asking the opposite of *Who can afford to be critical?* flips the script, dissolves the guilt, and equates experiences that initially might seem really disparate from one another, but in fact are closer than we think. Gijs' question settled for me the certainty that if interrogations like *"Who can afford to be critical?"* and *"What are we going to do?"* are carried out with conceit, then they are devoid of any radical character. Yes, they can be useful to examine the limits of our agency, our privileges and our power as designers, but if they are used to just judge others (or to constantly self-flaggelate ourselves), then this examination cannot be a fruitful one. The true radical project has to be one of solidarity, of embeddedness, of being *amongst* and not *above*. Of understanding why the other is behaving in such a way and why I'm behaving the way I am — something that is always socially, culturally and politically informed. To also be mindful of what we share, beyond what sets us apart. I hope to have laid down some pathways for that with this little book.

A NOTE ON HOW THE BOOK CAME TO BE

Part of the ethos behind this project consists in a commitment to transparency and honesty. And I was happy to find that Freek is equally committed to those same values, something you can easily check by going to Set Margins' website, where he lists all the steps of the new business plan and talks openly about financial responsibility, rates, ownership and collaboration. Following that, me and Freek thought it would be nice to share a bit about how this object got materialized.

First of all, I contacted Freek because I saw that he commented on a post Silvio Lorusso made on Instagram regarding the publishing of an excerpt from my thesis on *Other Worlds* (thank you Silvio!). Freek commented on it, and since I knew his work as an editor, I saw there an opportunity to contact him and see what we could do together. I was very well received (thank you Freek!) and so the plan to edit the fanzines together into a single publication started to form. From the get go, we decided that we would split all costs and all profits evenly. We're investing personal money into this: as I've mentioned already, I'm leaning on my parent's support as I'm still not earning enough money on my own to sustain myself, much less pay for editing a book, and Freek is also pulling from his personal finances in order to make this happen. Regarding contributions, this books also owes a lot to the kindness (and labor) of all the contributing authors which accepted to be part of it without asking for monetary compensation. It must also be mentioned that most of the time I spent on writing was within education and the time for post-production and redesign of the book was for free, as well as Freek's editorial advice, support in print and coordination.

We tried to look for ways in which we could get a nice-looking object while not spending too much money, and for that I counted on Freek's budgeting expertise, on his knowledge of print shops and editorial processes in general. We followed along, opting for an A5 format, which is still quite generous, and starting out by asking budgets for an all black-and-white publication. When the quotes came in, we both decided that we still had some lee-way to spend a bit more than what the budget mentioned. As such, we decided to go for a 5 color (4 PMS + black) printing, so we could do justice to the original silkscreen colors the covers of the fanzines used. In the end, we spent 1391€ each for the printing of 1200 copies, which amounts to a total of 2782€.

A NOTE ON WHAT THE BOOK LOOKS LIKE

For the graphic design, I had a simple principle in mind at first: having fun. You could also say that I went for such messy aesthetics in order to "mock" the visual trends that one can see in many Critical (Graphic) Design works. I wouldn't deny that. But it must be said that I also truly like those visual expressions. I truly appreciate them. And indeed, as Freek reminded me, the communication strategy the book employs does fit with the "multivocal" ethics of trying to get many people I like and respect together in one book, so that others out there can find their thoughts and their writings. These approaches to plurality through graphic design are already being explored by many talented designers nowadays. So I guess if there is mockery of some clichés (and there is, a bit), then I'm also mocking myself, and if there's appreciation, then it's directed outwards to many of the amazing practitioners that are experimenting with new ways of communicating, of including marginalized voices, and who have informed my taste in the past years.

This mockery, this "having fun", is partially a spontaneous method and partially also justified by a chapter of my thesis where I talked about "semiotic collapse:" the idea that aesthetics are so easily appropriated by capitalism that you can't say for sure whether x, y or z typeface, color or layout is *inherently* radical (or queer, or decolonial, or anticapitalist) or not. As Stuart Hall writes, *"What counts is the class struggle in and over culture. Almost every fixed inventory will betray us. Is the novel a 'bourgeois' form? The answer can only be historically provisional."* [4] So, criteria for choosing one typeface over another collapse, and all we're left with is *vibes*: going for what we think looks nice.

[4] Hall, S. (1994). Deconstructing the Popular. Cultural Theory and Popular Culture: A Reader, 442-53.

Still, just saying "I like it, it looks nice" can be seen as an expression of privilege in itself. That is because taste and aesthetic sensibility is, of course, socially and cullturally produced, so it's also never neutral. The turn towards expressive, maximalist, pluralist aesthetics in these Critical circles seems to be tied with a larger cultural questioning of the white, male, eurocentric legacy of the modernist project. And questioning this legacy is of the utmost importance, not only because it is a right for those who have been systemically excluded to be given an equal place for speaking, but also because there are real implications of not doing so for how discriminated groups see themselves and see (imagine/visualize) the world that they (we) could inhabit.

However, I still I think that there are real dangers in focusing too much on aesthetic exploration, as opposed to the material reality which underlies our designing. That is why (graphic) design's obsession with the agency that certain forms, shapes, layouts and typefaces inherently have can be seen, in my opinion, as quite hubristic. This stance can easily bypass the role of power and the question of who can afford to even be in the position where they can explore these aesthetics with their work. And it also can fall into tokenism, into leading people to believe that just because we are "seeing" more representation, that such issues are being tackled at the material level. But that isn't necessarily true, and often institutions and corporations can use such discourses (and visuals) as aesthetic shields for the continuation of extractive and exploitative practices.

COLOPHON

Set Margins' #11

Who can affort to be critical?
An inquiry into what we can't do alone, as designers, and into what we might be able to do together, as people.
Afonso Matos (Ed.)

ISBN: 978-90-832706-3-0

Editor: Afonso Matos
Contributing authors: Afonso Matos. Silvio Lorusso, J. Dakota Brown, Marianela D'Aprile, Somnath Bhatt, Danielle Aubert, Jack Henrie Fisher, Alan Smart, Greg Mihalko, Evening Class,
Memes from: @ethicaldesign69, criticalgraphicdesign.tumblr.com, @dank.lloyd.wright
Graphic design: Afonso Matos
Text editor: Afonso Matos, Pedro Serafim
Advisor: Freek Lomme / Set Margins'
Printer: AS Printon
Papers: UMKA color 300g + Perigraphica Natural Rough 90g
Fonts: Gap Sans by GrandChaos9000 / Garamon(d/t) by Paul Tubert / Cinzel by Nathanael Gama / Courier New by Howard Bud Kettler / Italianno by Robert Leuschke / IM FELL Double Pica Pro by Peter de Walpergen and Igino Marini / Hershey Noailles by Allen Vincent Hershey and Luuse / EB Garamond by Claude Garamont, Georg Duffner and Octavio Pardo / Helvetica Neue by Max Miedinger and Eduard Hoffman / Comic Sans by Vincent Connare / Happy Times at the IKOB by Matthias Hübner / League Gothic by Caroline Hadilaksono, Micah Rich and Tyler Finck / Arial (and Arial Narrow) by Robin Nicholas and Patricia Saunders / Aileron by Sora Sagano / Lusitana by Ana Paula Megda / Syne by Bonjour Monde, Lucas Descroix, George Triantafyllakos / CirrusCumulus by Clara Sambot / Marker Felt by Dieter Steffmann / Combine by Julie Patard / Forum by Denis Masharov / Compagnon by Chloé Lozano, Juliette Duhé, Léa Pradine, Sébastien Riollier, Valentin Papon / Lynda by Ariel Di Lisio and Alejandro Paul / OCR-PBI by Lise Brosseau and Antoine Gelgon / Utopia by Antoine Gelgon / Almendra by Ana Sanfelippo / Cianan-ur by feorag / Snell Roundhand by Matthew Carter / Authentic Sans by Christina Janus and Desmond Wong / Impact by Geoffrey Lee / Yatra One by Catherine Leigh Schmidt / Amarante by Karolina Lach / Quattrocento by Impallari Type / Not Courier Sans by Open Source Publishing

Made possible thanks to much free labor from both Freek and Afonso, as well as shared investment into print by both. Returns will be divided equally.

Special thanks to Freek Lomme, Silvio Lorusso, J. Dakota Brown, Marianela D'Aprile, Somnath Bhatt, Danielle Aubert, Jack Henrie Fisher, Alan Smart, Greg Mihalko, @ethicaldesign69, Inês Pinheiro, Vítor Serra, Pedro Lobo, Gert Staal, Simon Davies, Irene Stracuzzi, Mar Ginot Blanco, Sergi Casero, Joost Grootens, Els Kuijpers, Gemma Copeland, Sofia Rocha e Silva, Ben Kasum, Gijs de Boer, Maxime Benvenuto, to all my bachelor's teachers, to the whole Info Design 2022 class, to all my other dear friends from DAE, to my dear friends from FBAUL and from Portalegre, and of course to my mom, dad, grandma and grandpa.

This publication is licensed under a
Creative Commons Attribution-NonCommercial-ShareAlike
4.0 International Licence (CC BY-NC-SA 4.0).
To view a copy of this license, visit
https://creativecommons.org/licenses/by-nc-sa/4.0/

First edition, 2022

Set Margins'
www.setmargins.press

A big thank you to all my DAE friends that made this book possible.